TRANSPORT IN

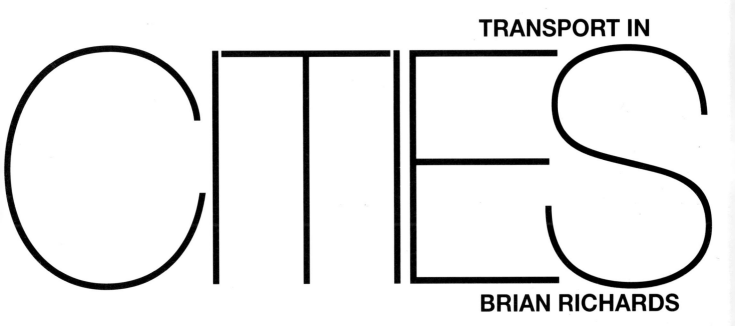

# CITIES

BRIAN RICHARDS

ARCHITECTURE
DESIGN AND
TECHNOLOGY
PRESS

Architecture Design and
Technology Press
128 Long Acre
London
WC2E 9AN

ISBN 1 85454 545 0

Copyright © Brian Richards 1990

First published 1990

British Library Cataloguing in
Publication Data
A CIP catalogue record for this book is
available from the British Library

Design: Jonathan Moberly

Text: 9.5/12pt Adobe Helvetica

Typeset and made up to page using
QuarkXpress on an Apple Macintosh II

Linotronic: Alphabet Set

Printed in Great Britain by
The Bath Press

## Acknowledgements

All the people and authorities who have helped provide information and
advice are too numerous to list in detail.

Special thanks to Francis Tibbalds who read the script and made
valuable suggestions; Margaret Heraty who advised on the chapter on
disabled people; Sandy Boyle who helped organise the typing; Robin
Rudolph who twice typed the script; and my wife Sandra Lousada who took
many of the photographs.

All illustrations not otherwise credited are courtesy of the author.

# CONTENTS

# PREFACE

*New Movement in Cities*, published in 1966, illustrated a range of interesting ideas for moving people over short distances that had been tried in the early part of the century. Twenty years ago was a time of white hot technology and a moon landing. It appeared then quite feasible that such systems as moving pavements could make it so easy to move within future city centres that conventional public transport and private cars would become outdated and irrelevant.

*Moving in Cities*, published in 1976, at the time of the energy crisis, included more conventional systems, as well as some advanced technology, including such systems as personal rapid transit – small tracked vehicles under computer control, which, at the press of a button, took a passenger directly to his or her required station. These were then being tried in the United States and Japan, and would be used in the same way as the lifts in any multi-storeyed building, but only for horizontal movement, and were paid for by the developments through which they ran.

Both books, however, avoided the issue of *traffic* in cities, and how to deal with it, in the mistaken belief that were public transport sufficiently good, people would use it and those with cars would leave them at home.

This book explores what methods are available today for restraining vehicular traffic, and the range of transport alternatives available. It suggests that a combination of measures, properly used, could lead to major environmental improvements in our cities and help make them places to enjoy.

*New Movement in Cities* (1966) Studio Vista, London; Reinhold, New York; Marsilio Editori, Padua and Callwey, Munich; (1968) Kajima, Tokyo; (1969) Bonniers, Stockholm.
*Moving in Cities* (1976) Studio Vista, London and Westview Press, Boulder, Colorado.

# 1
# TRANSPORT AND THE CITY

Moving around in cities is becoming increasingly difficult. As the pressure for homes and working spaces grows, so too does the demand for roads and other transport. Roads and parking spaces already occupy a large proportion of the land within cities – up to 30 per cent of its area in Europe and often more than 50 per cent in North America. This infrastructure is an essential part of the fabric of the city, and the continuing pressure on it has contributed to a steady deterioration in the quality of life – often making cities no longer places to enjoy.

Only in recent years has the public become more concerned with the deterioration of the environment – usually when this affects the area where they live, and particularly when new road proposals are made which may affect their homes, even requiring them to be demolished. This has become one of the most controversial factors in city planning and reconstruction.

In compact cities of 1 million or less the problems are less acute. Travel distances to work or to shop are shorter. Transport issues are easier to resolve in practical terms and the solutions are easier to implement, because, with one central planning authority, strategies can be more easily made and implemented through the political process. City-dwellers are more aware of what is going on and feel able to have some say in the decisions made. Moreover, the decisions can be more quickly implemented and, if they are the right solutions, can improve the image of the city in a shorter space of time.

In large cities, with a more diffuse political control, professional departments dealing with different aspects of transport may make decisions which are uncoordinated and lead to a steady deterioration of travel conditions and the environment. Nowhere is this becoming more apparent than in Greater London.

One of the principal factors in London, apart from the lack of an overall planning strategy, is the problem of population growth. All cities grow. Decisions have to be made when to call a halt. The 'green belt' around London, for example, however much under attack, fortunately persists as a mechanism to control sprawl and outward growth. But, in addition, a strategy for planning new growth points outside the city boundary is required. The New Towns around London attempted this, but to be effective required to be interlinked by high-speed rail such as has been done in Holland's Randstad. In addition, new growth points have to be developed within the city boundary and existing worn-out suburbs gradually renewed at higher densities.

This chapter explores some of the principal factors which concern transport planning in the city – how land uses relate to transport; the role of public transport; and dealing with congestion, the private car and pollution. All these are transport-related factors which affect the quality of life in present-day cities.

## LAND-USE PLANNING

This is the domain of the local planning authority which, in Britain, is responsible for formulating a development plan for that part of the city it controls, a plan which is then published and agreed democratically by the public and its representatives. Planners must look ahead far enough to decide how an area might be allowed to change in the future, to allow unforeseen factors to be incorporated. For example, if the city plan encourages a local centre to increase in scale, it must also consider how its growth can be accommodated. Previously, many planning decisions were road-orientated. New road-building was thought to be an essential requirement to deal with 'traffic generation'. Often a low priority was placed on how public transport might be improved to serve an area. These aspects, which are explored below, are typical of the problems which have to be overcome in dealing with transport for different parts of the city – industrial, shopping, commercial and residential areas.

### Industrial areas

There is a case for those industries now within cities, which are generators of large numbers of freight vehicles, to be resited where land is cheap and adequate roads exist or can be readily improved. This may occur naturally as land values increase closer to the city centre and industry moves out to cheaper land. Direct access to the rail network is desirable for freight, and good access by public transport is essential, if land is not to be wasted on private car parking. Inducements should be made to employers to provide their own minibus services to ensure that their employees can reach their workplaces – and car-pooling (see The Car) can also be similarly encouraged. Closer in to the city centre, smaller industrial estates should be provided for in the development plan, capable of being

**Figure 1**  (above) Computer Commuter is a ride-sharing service run by Commuter Transportation Services in Los Angeles and serves around 40,000 drivers a year with car- and van-pooling, using a computer to match up passengers, and serving around 17 per cent of commuter trips in Los Angeles. More and more people are using car-pooling as parking subsidies decrease, with in one company 59 per cent of employees using the car-pool.
Courtesy Computer-Commuter.

**Figure 2**  (below) The 3M Centre in Minnesota began Commute-a-van in 1973 with six vans, now risen to 105 vans providing door-to-door transport for over 1000 employees, and freeing 730 parking spaces as well as reducing vehicles on the surrounding roads. Due to increasing congestion from car traffic, and in spite of heavy investment in roads, local authorities in California and other states in the USA now require developers in suburban areas to show how they plan to provide access for car commuters before allowing them to build. Contributions are required towards road improvements and space has to be allocated in parking areas for car-pooling. Some freeways allow bus-priority lanes to be used as well by 'high occupancy vehicles', cars which have three passengers.
Courtesy 3M Minnesota.

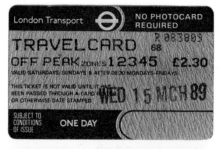

**Figure 3** *Travelcards given to employees as an alternative to subsidising company cars are preferable, provided public transport is good enough, and so reduce the pressures on road space at peak periods.*
Courtesy London Regional Transport.

**Figure 4** *Privately-run minibuses could be provided to serve small industrial areas as a requirement given by local authorities allowing access to the nearest light rail or express bus stop. This view is of an interchange station on the Newcastle Metro.*
Courtesy Tyne and Wear Passenger Transport Executive.

related to bus or tram routes, and only limited paid parking provided. Employers should be required by the local authority to show how they are encouraging workers to share cars, or use public transport and, where appropriate, this could be part of the leasing requirements laid down by the local authority. Parking controls would be required in the neighbourhoods surrounding a factory estate to avoid an invasion of workers' cars. Free bus or train 'Travelcards', rather than company cars, should be provided by employers as an inducement to workers not to drive to work, and for those without cars. Such a strategy, in lower density areas, would be aimed at reducing the pressure for more road space. They are policies which should be introduced for all development outside the centre, and are used in North America today (Cervero, 1984), for example in California, where road space is already saturated, to reduce the demand for more road building.

## Shopping centres

In Europe, there is continuous pressure from developers for shopping centres to be sited outside towns and cities on green-field sites, alongside motorways or large roads, where land is cheap. Such developments have grown in North America to form regional centres often serving 500,000 people within 20 minutes' driving time. Many are well-designed with offices, shopping, sports and leisure facilities and even some residential development. Regional centres have developed quickly. For example, the North Parkway area outside Dallas has quadrupled in size in six years and by 1990 is expected to rival downtown Dallas in office space (Orski, 1987). Yet they contain an air of unreality about them. They are quite unlike the life of downtown areas. They lack a live-in population and are often unrelated to the surrounding areas and not served by public transport. Access is solely by private cars, forming a sea of parking surrounding each centre. Such developments are now being built in Europe and contribute little to improving life in cities. They simply avoid the problems of building in cities and use up valuable rural land. Only in one case, at Milton Keynes, has a shopping centre been used to form the centre of a new city, with an eventual population of 200,000. Here residential areas are situated within a ten-minute walk of the centre, which is also connected to a railway station, with offices, all within walking distance or a short bus ride of one another. This example has some of the qualities of urbanity which shopping centres should have in the context of an existing city. Integrated with the grain of surrounding streets and close, or part of existing centres where they would provide an alternative to the 'strip development' now being built on so many roads leading into existing cities. So placed that they would be well-served by public transport routes – bus, tram or rail – and place less reliance on access by the private car. These developments would be accessible to people on foot or cycle from existing residential areas surrounding them. They would require an improved public transport system rather than an enlarged road system to serve them, and parking would be provided only for those cars which the existing roads could carry. But the concentration of facilities would justify this expenditure and prove in the long run to be far less costly than any new road-building.

## Offices

In addition to improvements to existing centres there are wasteland areas, within cities, now often occupied by redundant railway lines or factories, which are potential areas for new growth. One example of this is now being planned at King's Cross, north London, where it is intended to build mixed development, offices, high-density residential flats, workshops and shops all located within walking distance of two mainline railways, three underground lines and bus routes, and surrounded on three sides by an existing residential area.

Such inner city development could help relieve pressure on the central area, by making use of the existing public transport network infrastructure and improving it, at least partly at the developer's expense. However, it still provides, in the proposed plans, all-day parking for seven per cent of the workforce, commuter-parking, rather than short-wait parking, at the request of the local authority. This is in the belief that the measure will discourage commuters from parking in the surrounding neighbourhoods. Such parking provision could be provided, as in Munich, on sites at the periphery of London and so avoid the need for road improvements which will be necessary not only locally but on radial roads serving them.

## Residential areas

It is important to retain and expand residential areas close to the central areas of a city and to encourage more people to live within walking distance of their offices and to shops, to ensure that the city retains a live-in population. For example, Toronto built around 10,000 new housing units in 1976, mostly for relatively high-income households, without children, in the central area. These developments, with a population of 15,000 people, were balanced by an office growth of 7.5 million square feet, in the same period. A sample survey of residents (Stewart and Mihalcin 1983) showed that 35 per cent walked to work in summer and 29 per cent did so in winter, and that 70 per cent of all trips were made to work in the central area.

Within existing residential areas the retention of local shops is important, along with the provision of other essential facilities for residents within walking distance of homes. Many local centres could be expanded to contain small offices, workshops and studios, provided that parking spaces are strictly limited to short-term use. New housing can also contain provision for workspace, and in London and elsewhere several schemes have been built and have proved very successful.

## Telecommunications

The developments in computers, electronic mail and fax machines have encouraged some firms to relocate a proportion of their working

**Figure 5** Scarborough, Ontario, a new suburb north of Toronto, estimated to serve half a million people, has developed its centre around the new ALRT light-rail system, whose station is directly connected to the shopping centre. This degree of integration of public transport with development is an advance on most other centres in North America, although the extent of parking, the way it has been planned, and the geometry of the roads serving it is problematic. Peripheral parking could have allowed for a more dense development closer to the station.
Courtesy Township of Scarborough. Photo Mykusz.

**Figure 6**  *London's Docklands has developed rapidly in five years, partly due to the construction of the Light Railway, regarded by developers as an essential transport link to the City. The system is shown here, running elevated across the docks and the Canary Wharf site where a new enlarged station is under construction.*
*As seen, the road infrastructure is minimal and new road-building likely to be soon congested. The extension to the Underground railway now being planned, initially rejected by the Government as too expensive, will be essential to serve the rapidly expanding transport needs of the area.*
Courtesy London Docklands Development Corporation.

staff away from central area locations to sub-centres where rents can be halved. Experiments have been made by telephone companies in France and Denmark to set up satellite centres at the periphery of a centre, where workers from different organisations can share a single office and use the computer facilities provided which are linked to their parent companies (Kinsman, 1987). Home-based working is, however, more usual and particularly well-suited to mothers raising a family, who are provided with a computer and modem linked to their office base. All these changes in workplaces, however small now, are likely to increase as the technology improves and will reduce the need to travel long distances to work.

## PUBLIC TRANSPORT

European cities have grown up around roads and railways radiating from the historic centres where the major business activities are concentrated. North American cities, except for those with established centres as in New York or Chicago, have developed around roads, often on a widely spaced network of freeways, resulting in a dispersal of workplaces away from the centres. In radial cities public transport continues to serve a high proportion of trips to the centre. In non-radial cities the car provides the main system of transport – together with buses, for those without cars.

In all cities the problems lie in the shortage of road space and how it can be used to the best advantage. If cities are to survive the continuing growth of car ownership and use, then, rather than building more roads, existing road space must be rationed, and drivers of vehicles using road space in congested areas must pay for the congestion they cause to others at peak hours of the day. The exception to this would be the essential services, buses, public service vehicles, and cars for disabled people. These ideas have been around now for over 20 years (Roth, 1967) but only in recent years have they become accepted as inevitable, with increased recognition of the extent of car ownership and congestion.

In Singapore, a system of tolls was introduced in 1975 along all roads entering the central area. This obliges car drivers not carrying three passengers to pay a fee for entering. Daily, weekly or monthly tickets are pre-bought and displayed in the car windows for random checking by police at the tolls. The system has successfully reduced the number of cars entering the central area by around 50 per cent, with drivers transferring on to the new bus fleet that was specially

**Figure 7**

*Home-based working, made easier by developments in computers, electronic mail and fax machines. Government statistics estimate that 25 per cent of the UK working population might be working at home by 1994 and so reduce the need for daily travel to work.*
Courtesy Lousada.

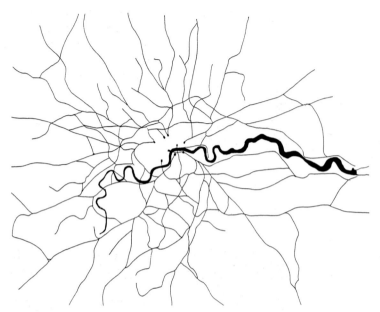

**Figure 8** London's radial rail network. Responsible for the pattern of growth and densities and carrying major flows of passengers to workplaces in the centre. Some lines, or part of them, particularly cross-city lines could be used in the future as part of light rail links.

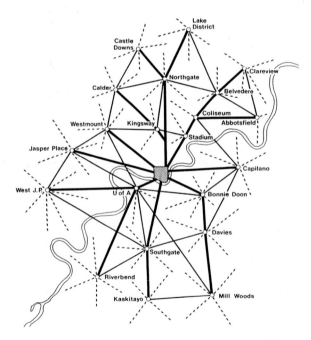

**Figure 9** Edmonton, Alberta. A typical North American city where 75 per cent of work trips are orbital to points outside the central area, in this case well-served by a unique bus system, reducing the need for commuting by car.
Courtesy City of Edmonton.

**Figure 10** *Traffic restraint in the centre of many cities is badly needed and Singapore introduced tolls at 28 points around its central area in 1975, operating at peak hours, effectively reducing the number of cars entering by around 50 per cent.*
Courtesy Armstrong-Wright

**Figure 11** *Two types of license are used in Singapore for daily or monthly use, purchased at booths near to the main roads. Licenses are displayed in the cars' side windows and checked by roadside police. Cars with three or more people are allowed in free, company cars charged at double rates and taxis at half rates. Freight vehicles are free.*
Courtesy Armstrong-Wright

provided, or the Underground (see Road-pricing and controls: area licensing). In Hong Kong, a successful pilot study was undertaken, from 1983 to 1985, of an electronic road pricing system. This used a small box, an electronic number plate, fitted to the underside of all cars which would enter the central area. As a car passed over a loop set at intervals in the road, a computer checked and recorded the number of the car, and the driver would be billed monthly for the length of the journeys made at peak hours in the congested central area.

Both systems are aimed at freeing road space through pricing, to reduce the use of roads by certain classes of vehicles and to encourage car drivers to switch to public transport. The reduction of traffic within a central area will then allow the road space that is freed

**Figure 12** *Hanover's Ustra light-rail system has car parking at its terminal stations at ground level, around which the tram loops, to allow for direct cross-platform access. This convenient arrangement makes the system equally attractive for shoppers and commuters.* Courtesy USTRA

from cars to be used by buses and cycles, or for an overall improvement to the environment to be made, by widening pavements, planting trees or creating more pedestrian areas.

The importance of providing good public transport becomes vital if road-pricing is to be acceptable to a public, and politicians, who are increasingly orientated towards cars. The Hamburg transport authority, HBB, for example, accepts that the road lobby is powerful and that it would be hard to reduce the present 30,000 car spaces within the city centre. However, this number has now been frozen, and the authority is concentrating on providing new multi-storeyed park-and-ride points outside the centre, connected directly by lift to platform level on the S-Bahn rapid transit system. Paris provides parking spaces for 100,000 cars adjoining stations and high speed Réseau Express Régional lines which cross the city centre from the suburbs. This system is popular with motorists wishing to avoid clogged motorways. However, park-and-ride is expensive to provide and wasteful of valuable land. Taking a further German example, Hanover provides a very efficient ride-and-ride system at peripheral stations where feeder buses are computerised to arrive at stations to coincide with the arrival of trams on the light-rail system (see Interchanges).

Once an increase in road space is brought about through restraint on car use, buses are able to move faster, to time, on exclusive bus lanes (see Buses). Outside the central area, privately-run minibuses

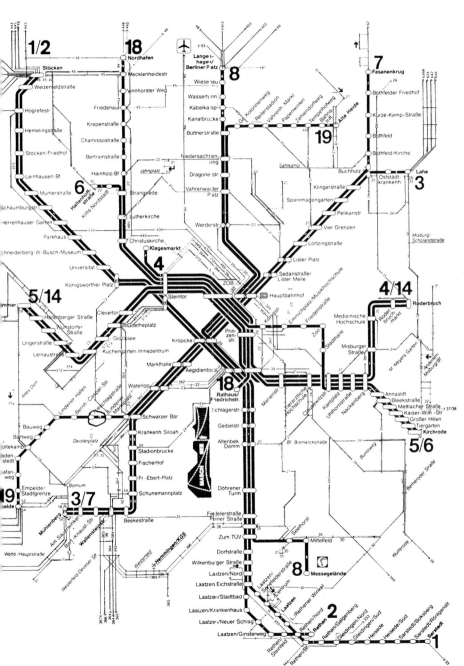

**Figure 13** Diagram showing Hanover's four light rail routes, a total of 98 km (58 miles), of which 13 km (8 miles) are in tunnel, the remainder on separate rights of way at surface-level outside the city centre. Bus routes, shown in solid line, allow interchange at 24 stations. Courtesy USTRA

**Figure 14** A shopping delivery service run by USTRA every Saturday in the centre of Hanover. Shoppers can store purchases in cartons at a depot in the pedestrian area for a small fee, or have them delivered to their homes for under £2 ($3). Up to 2500 people a day have used the system, an estimated 10 per cent of public transport passengers. Photo USTRA.

could be licensed to run on crosstown routes, as well as to act as a feeder system to rapid-rail stations, or to serve local centres. The proposals suggested for road-pricing in most cities could be implemented within a period of three to five years, given the political will. In that time, as was done in Singapore, an enlarged bus fleet could be introduced, with the essential bus lanes built and the improvements made at road junctions to traffic lights to give them priority over other vehicles. Longer-term improvements would then be made to upgrade those routes carrying large flows of commuters, to take guided buses, or to construct new light-rail systems.

## Paying for public transport

There are few cities where public transport does not have to be subsidised. This is principally to keep the system running, but also to provide an affordable service for people with a wide range of incomes. Increasing car ownership and use has generally proved unprofitable for bus operation, in particular, where the spiral of increasing road congestion and poor bus reliability has led people to purchase cars and use them. Radial rail trips, however, remain attractive, even for car owners, because of high journey speeds and reliability. They are therefore profitable. New systems, such as minibuses or radio-controlled taxis, are often more profitable if run by private companies, in suburban areas, possibly with subsidy from the local authority. Hamburg, for example, subsidises private taxi companies to run evening services from their stations, at less cost than a conventional bus service and giving a door-to-door service.

Fixed-track systems – principally 'rapid transit' and, to a lesser extent, 'light rail' – require heavy capital investment in construction, which has normally to be written off by the funding authority. These systems are profitable, if the flows of people are sufficient, but still require subsidies of from 25 per cent (in London) to 50 per cent (in Hamburg) to run. Fares for all public transport systems require to be set at a level where the maximum number of passengers remain attracted to the system and many authorities favour 'Travelcards' which are pre-bought on a weekly or monthly basis, and allow for unlimited travel with interchange between bus and rail.

Fixed-track systems have, in recent years, been seen to act as a profitable way of increasing land values. In Hong Kong substantial use was made of air rights development over stations. In London's Docklands the capital costs of a 7.7 km (4.8 mile) extension to the light-rail system with ten stations will be paid for by the enhanced land values of

**Figure 15** *In Paris over 40 per cent of the bus routes are on exclusive lanes free from other traffic. Many buses are fitted with 'transponders' an electronic device which operates lights in their favour. New tickets called 'Cartes Orange' which allow for interchange have resulted in a 36 per cent increase in passengers using buses, many transferring from the Méro.* Photo RATP.

the areas the stations will serve. Developers now see such systems as vital to the rents they can charge for offices, which are based on the proximity of a station, and the developer will often contribute substantially towards the capital cost of the system (see Rail).

The subsidies for running public transport may be partly found through a special tax on employers, such as is done in French cities of 100,000 people and over, where a tax is imposed on those firms with ten or more employees, the *versement transports*, who pay, for example, in Paris 2 per cent of their salaries towards public transport. In Paris this meets around 50 per cent of the cost of subsidising transport, which still requires a 40–50 per cent subsidy, compared with London, where 80 per cent of operating costs are met from the fare box. In West Germany, fuel oil is taxed and is used to finance local roads and transport networks such as many of the U-Bahn and S-Bahn in the larger cities (Simpson, 1988).

## ROADS

New road-building in existing cities has been a political issue for many years. The road-building lobby, which is powerful, sees roads as being a tangible solution to congestion and 'what the public want'. The anti-road lobby sees them as only encouraging more traffic, increasing congestion and, in urban areas, losing homes (Hamer, 1987).

The building of radial roads in London, planned 20 years before, largely ended with the construction of a 6.4 km (4 mile) elevated road, called 'Westway' and completed in 1970, which resulted in an estimated 38 per cent increase in traffic in central London (Plowden, 1980). The construction of this road provoked a storm of protest from residents living alongside who have since been partly rehoused. In other cities in the world there have been similar experiences. San Francisco's Western Freeway and Toronto's Spadina Expressway were both bitterly opposed by the public but, unlike the London experience, led to the construction of new rapid-transit systems (Leavitt, 1970).

Today the concept of improving radial roads has been largely replaced by one of building orbital or tangential roads. However, the arguments previously used about improving traffic flow and increasing mobility have now dramatically changed. Such roads are now presented as 'relief' roads, a way of 'improving' the environment through which they pass, disregarding the question of traffic generation. If tangential or relief roads are built, they have to be acceptable environmentally in the areas through which they pass. Dr Martin

*Figure 16*  London's Westway, an elevated radial motorway completed in 1970 resulted in an estimated 38 per cent increase in traffic entering central London with no environmental benefits, and was opposed by residents living alongside. In other cities, notably Toronto, opposition to motorway construction has led to new rapid transit being constructed.

*Figure 17*  Piecemeal orbital motorway schemes in London are being contested by action groups on the grounds that they will encourage more traffic to enter the city.

Mogridge suggests, in an important study for Docklands in east London (Mogridge, 1987), that rather than build motorways for mixed traffic, single-track two-lane roads could be built in certain corridors, either in tunnel or in cut and semi-cover, in order to minimize the destruction of property. These could be toll roads, restricted to a speed of 80 km/h (50 mph), available for freight vehicles and express buses

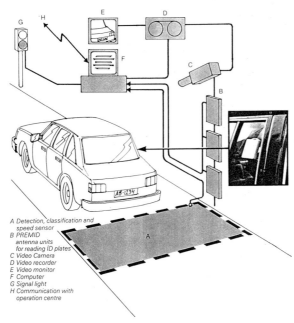

A Detection, classification and
  speed sensor
B PREMID
  antenna units
  for reading ID plates
C Video Camera
D Video recorder
E Video monitor
F Computer
G Signal light
H Communication with
  operation centre

**Figure 18** *Automatic toll systems are being used in Alesund, Norway, and experimentally at toll bridges in the United States. Regular drivers purchase an electronic 'smart card' form their banks on a regular basis, which are placed in the car window and read by roadside antennae, without stopping. Cars with out-of-date cards are monitored on videotape.*

**Figure 19** *Car parks or residential areas can use the same device. A housing estate in Greenwich, London, has installed the system issuing cards to residents who can enter, and so prevents commuters and shoppers using their parking space.*
Courtesy Philips Scientific & Industrial Division.

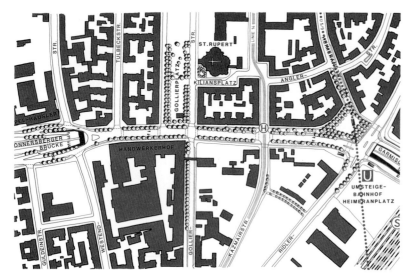

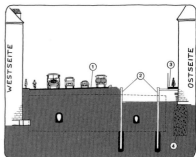

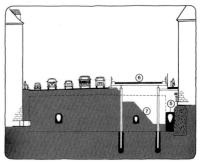

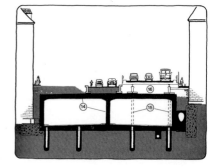

**Figures 20, 21** *Plan and sections showing the construction procedure of Munich's Trappentreustrasse, part of the middle ring road built as a result of popular demand to divert traffic from the inner city and offload it in a tunnel through part of a residential area. The cost was five times greater than that of demolishing and rebuilding the houses elsewhere, but the construction problems were accepted by the local residents resulting in an improvement in the street environment. The two tunnels built have used up the state's subsidy for roadbuilding in Munich for the next ten years.* Courtesy Baureferat der Landeshauptstadt, Munich

at peak periods, or at off-peak periods for private cars.

Such 'controlled toll roads' could be privately financed and use the new electronic 'smart cards', for access through simple toll barriers, without stopping. Cars would use separate lanes and be held back in the same way as they are now, at the entry lanes to some motorways in the United States where sensors detect when space is available and allow vehicles to enter. Exit points would be at 3–6.5 km (2–4 mile) intervals and the roads would terminate at the peripheral motorway system. Tunnelled roads would, however, be expensive, and are difficult to ventilate. Tunnelling of a section of ring road, the *Trappentreustrasse* – a six-lane road in a Munich suburb – has cost five times more than demolishing homes and building new houses elsewhere (OECD, 1988). But bitter opposition to more surface motorway construction in Munich, following the halting of the inner ring road, has meant that the city has voted to make tunnelled roads a requirement in certain areas, to reduce their environmental impact.

Not all 'controlled toll roads' would need to be tunnelled. Some would take over existing surface level roads, or disused railways, if environmentally acceptable. However, the important idea of toll roads is that they could be priced at a level high enough to keep out car commuters, and would remove from existing main roads those freight vehicles not serving the immediate area. This would allow improvements to take place on the existing main road network, which would still carry local traffic, including buses. Some roads joining the main roads would be closed, as a result of environmental 'cells' being introduced to residential areas on either side of the main roads, as discussed below.

## CONGESTION

All cities suffer from congestion at certain times of the day, and the measures taken to reduce this are political ones and will, to some extent, depend on the finances available and whether the congestion is serious enough to cause businesses to move out of the city and for trade and land values to drop.

Congestion on roads in city centres causes traffic speeds to stabilise and occasionally 'grind to a halt'. In London, for example, traffic speeds have not changed much over the last 40 years (Mogridge, 1985) and have stabilised at an average of 20 km/h (12 mph). This is due to a number of factors. Many car drivers have transferred to trains, or to the Underground system, because they are quicker and traffic management measures, together with sophisticated systems of area-wide traffic control, cannot squeeze any further capacity out of the road network.

Congestion on rail systems at peak hours similarly occurs in most cities and only when overcrowding becomes actually dangerous for passengers, and a political issue, are measures introduced to ease the problem. This will normally be done in as economic a way as possible to give value for money, because the transport system normally has spare capacity at off-peak times. For example, new rolling stock under computer control, combined with new signalling, will improve the frequency of trains and reduce headways. Trains may also be made longer, to increase their capacity, but this requires the expensive extension of platforms. New lines may be built to provide relief to existing ones. For example, suburban lines, now terminating at peripheral stations, may be extended across the city (as in Paris with the Métro Régional) and so avoid the need for interchanging.

In contrast, new roads built in parts of a city may produce only temporary relief to other parts of the network. They then attract so much traffic that they too become congested, causing traffic speeds to drop. Toll roads, by using the pricing mechanism, may restrict the type of traffic to freight, for example, and help resolve this problem.

Restraint on car use, which would reduce road congestion, could be made by area licensing or road-pricing (see Road-pricing and controls: area licensing). This would, through the level at which prices were set, deter car driving and allow for certain classes of vehicle to cross the cordon area or drive within the centre without charge. The road space freed from cars would then be available for use by buses – providing bus lanes on heavily-used corridors, and equipping them with devices to allow them to turn traffic lights in their favour (see Buses). This would allow for increases in bus speeds and, with more buses provided, a consequent increase in capacity.

A reduction in demand for public transport at peak periods could be encouraged by introducing higher fares at peak periods than at off-peak, and could mean introducing a two-tier system of 'Travelcards' (in London) or 'Cartes Oranges' (in Paris). Offices and workplaces, as now, would be encouraged to adjust further their working hours by using 'Flexitime' to avoid the peak periods.

Walking can be encouraged, rather than using public transport, for short trips – particularly in city centres – by providing better conditions for pedestrians, and wider pavements can be constructed where traffic volumes have been reduced. Finally, the encouragement of street life and traffic-free areas with small shops, cafés and bars could do much to keep people downtown in the evening peak hours and so avoid the worst travel periods.

## ENVIRONMENTAL FACTORS

The decisions made on how we move around the city affect the overall quality of life in the city. The problems caused by traffic – for example, its noise, and the level of fumes generated – are all critical, because of the impact they make on the environment. While the problems vary according to the situation, those concerning traffic, its speed and the kind of vehicles, all affect the nature of the street and the well-being of all the people using it.

**Figure 22** *A pedestrian street in the centre of Hamburg, part of a continuous network crossing the city centre.*

*Figure 23* Standard pavement detail in central Copenhagen, showing subdivisions using granite setts.

*Figure 24* Laying granite setts on a sand bed in Stroget, Copenhagen. A finish much-liked by city planners, it is however rough and hard to walk on until worn smooth. The quality of the detail is an important factor in any successful pedestrian street. Pavements must be well-designed and attention paid to lighting, tree-planting and the provision of seating. Above all, they must be well maintained.

## Pedestrian streets

One of the most significant improvements to the street environment in the last 20 years has been the development of traffic-free pedestrian areas (see Walking). These have successfully eliminated the noise level and fumes from vehicles. With the possibility of accidents also eliminated, there is an increase in the well-being of the pedestrian, who can enjoy a higher standard of environment, and more people will use the street. More important, shops and cafés add much to this, and benefit too from the increased trade they enjoy.

One approach, adopted in at least 25 per cent of German cities, has been to introduce traffic-free areas where only public transport is permitted to use the street. Pavements are widened and landscaped in shopping streets, and only buses or trams cross the pedestrian areas. Noise levels can remain a problem. In Portland Oregon, 175 buses an hour on its busway produced a noise reading of 75 dBA and eventually required a modified bus fleet. In other cities, such as Grenoble, traffic-free streets have been paved over in the centre with granite setts, and new tram lines provided. Pedestrian safety is a problem in both kinds of street, as there is a tendency for people to walk at random across the street. In Philadelphia's Chestnut Street, with 120 buses an hour in each direction, this became such a problem that marked crossing points were introduced (UMTA, 1979).

*Figure 25*  Philadelphia's Chestnut Street Transitway runs for twelve city blocks and carries around 45 buses an hour in each direction, previously used by 12,000 vehicles a day. With carefully detailed street furniture and special street lighting, the improved environment has stabilised pedestrian use, generally increasing it. Retail sales have marginally increased as a result of the upgrading. Some transit malls carry many more buses: that at Portland, Oregon was used by 150 buses an hour, requiring specially modified buses to reduce the noise level, since replaced by light rail and resulting in a cleaner environment.

Main through traffic
Main local road
Local street
Pedestrian area
One-way street
One-way street and cyclists.

**Figure 26**  *A dense residential neighbourhood in the centre of Copenhagen where roads are privately owned. The environmental cell concept has been used to keep through traffic on the peripheral roads while the inner roads and streets have been made one-way for access, some of which have cycle lanes or have been made into pedestrian-only streets, safe for children to play in. On-street parking is restricted and off-street parking is provided for 700 cars.*
Courtesy City of Copenhagen.

Generally people prefer pedestrian-only streets to be free from all vehicles (Stewart, 1979), although public transport must be readily available, either on parallel streets or crossing the pedestrian street at right angles.

## Environmental areas

These usually refer to residential areas of around 1 km square (1/2–3/4 mile), bounded on all sides by main roads. Within the 'environmental area' simple changes to existing roads are made, such as by making them one-way, or by closing some roads entering the main roads to create a 'maze', aimed at eliminating through traffic 'rat-running' through the area, while allowing internal local traffic to circulate. In some areas of German and Dutch cities (see Walking), 'traffic calming' measures have been introduced where, rather than creating a 'maze' of one-way roads, changes are made to road widths, to keep out large vehicles, and these changes are combined with street bumps, which slow vehicles down to 15 km/h (9mph). Street junctions are often modified and pavements widened, to reduce the danger fo pedestrians crossing. These improvements have been popular with residents in German towns, where discussions are held on their parking requirements and street design, before the schemes are implemented and have proved to be effective in reducing accidents and traffic noise levels, by reducing vehicle speeds.

*Figure 27* Bond Street, London. View of a partial street closure aimed at eliminating rat-running by vehicles, a street which should have been closed to traffic long ago.
Photo Lousada.

## Main road network

A strategy which creates pedestrian streets or environmental areas can result in some increased traffic on surrounding roads. However, there is, if anything, an over-cautious approach by traffic authorities before implementing such schemes experimentally. In many cases, given time, the displaced traffic will find alternative routes or be accommodated on the existing roads. For example, in Britain, in Norwich, where one of the first shopping streets to be pedestrianised was used by 560 cars per hour at peak periods before street closure, an increase of only 20 per cent in traffic was observed on the streets immediately adjacent after closure (OECD, 1974).

Generally a more inflexible approach could, with advantage, be adopted. Sir Colin Buchanan, for example, frequently advocated the 'sandbag approach' which could allow for experiments with street closure to assess results before a final irrevocable decision is made. For main roads already carrying heavy traffic, but with spare capacity, the vehicles displaced from environmental areas on the roads may cause an imperceptible change in noise level. If the road is to be turned into a 'freight road' (see Freight) the noise level would change, and special consideration for residents living along the road would certainly be required. For example, in Paris, householders living adjoining the inner ring road have their flats sound-proofed when the noise level

**Figure 28** *Earl's Court, London. Temporary barriers opposite the busy Underground station. Although reducing the capacity of the road, these give added safety for pedestrians crossing. There is a real need for temporary schemes such as this to be tried in cities which once they are seen not to create 'gridlock' elsewhere can then be made permanent.*

measures 70 dBA at the façade. Compensation may, in fact, prove to be the fairest policy for those owners of property where land values have decreased because of increases in traffic flows following the creation of environmental areas.

The technical problem of how pedestrians can cross busy main roads is frequently discussed. Solutions involving subways are intensely disliked, particularly by women, as are overbridges, both of which require ramps for disabled people. Only in exceptional circumstances are these solutions acceptable. Alternatively, crossing all streets, except those carrying heavy and fast traffic, such as outer ring roads, can be done by pedestrians at light-controlled crossings. This requires discipline, to wait for lights to change, but remains the best solution. Of particular interest is the scale of pedestrian crossings used in German cities. Often these are 6–10 metres (20–35 feet) wide – the width of the pedestrian streets on either side.

This chapter has provided a wide overview of transport-related problems in present-day cities. The following chapters explore the range of systems discussed in more detail.

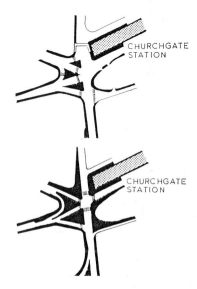

**Figure 29** *Churchgate station, Bombay, India. A footbridge formerly used by 70,000 commuters an hour during peak periods. The footbridge was inadequate to meet the load, taking 5 minutes to cross, and difficult for disabled people.* Courtesy Lousada

**Figure 31** *View after closure of the bridge. The scheme took only 3 months to implement has reduced accidents by 27 per cent and reduced crossing times to one minute. Only the bridge remains, as a source of advertising revenue.* Courtesy BMRDA. Consultant Brian Richards.

**Figure 30** *The station occurs at a busy street junction which was widened to improve turning by vehicles. Following a turning ban on all vehicles except buses the bridge was closed to pedestrians.* Courtesy BMRDA

Walking is an essential part of movement in cities. Within city centres it is done largely from choice, as the easiest and quickest, or most pleasant, means of moving over short distances. Walking is slow, depending on the kind of trip, age and numbers of others walking. Estimated walking speeds can be around 4.7 km/h (2.9 mph) for a shopping trip up to a speed of 7.3 km/h (4.5 mph) for a journey to work in mixed traffic (Pushkarev and Zupan, 1975).

Within dense central areas the distances people will walk vary and can depend on the environment and on how used they are to walking. Some estimate an acceptable walking trip of about 300–500 metres (1/4 mile) as the norm, such as from an underground station to the office; many will from choice walk much further, if it means they avoid interchanging on public transport. In general, people using public transport have to walk further than those who travel by car. In a study made of 700 people in Sweden (Lovemark, 1970) it was found that a walking trip made in a more interesting and undisturbed environment might be 30 per cent longer, or, given a generous pavement width and an interesting environment, this might increase to 50 per cent longer.

## PEDESTRIAN STREETS

The single most important improvement to walking conditions in city centres in the last 25 years has been the introduction of pedestrian streets free from traffic. These have often been extended as networks over the centre, to connect to the major generators of pedestrian movement, the railways or underground stations, such as in Hamburg or Cologne. They have been particularly successful in fine historic streets, where the quality of the environment and degree of safety experienced has made them areas to enjoy. Most successful examples are those where the quality of streetscape detail has been well considered. German costs, for example, can be DM 200–400 per square metre (£49–£103 per square yard) for landscaping, which includes:

1 A high quality of paving, under which all the services have been usually relaid.
2 New street lighting designed to a human scale.
3 Landscaping including trees, planting and fountains.

**Figure 32** *Munich's Old City Hall built in the 15th century and the principal square, Marienplatz, pedestrianized in 1972 prior to the Olympic Games. It is paved in granite slabs laid on concrete to allow for on-street deliveries at limited periods. Most underground services were relaid following construction of the S-Bahn below this square.*
Courtesy Baureferat der Landeshauptstadt, Munich.

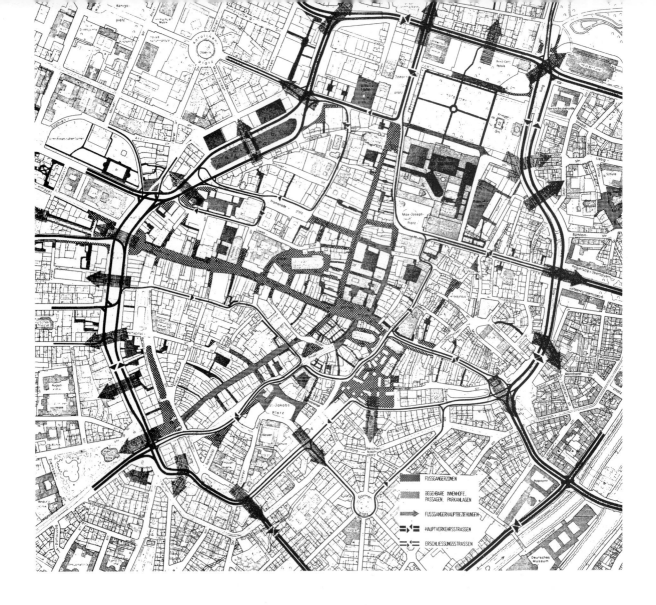

**Figure 33** Plan of Munich's central area showing tram routes at the periphery and the extent of the pedestrian area. Munich, a city of 1.3 million people, was one of the earliest to use pedestrian areas. The inner ring road, shown at the bottom, was only partly built and was stopped for environmental reasons. Recent policies rely on outer roads and peripheral parking to keep out cars, and excellent public transport. Courtesy Baureferat der Landeshauptstadt, Munich.

Factors of urban scale and land use are also important, such as the width of the street and quality of buildings above eye level, the spaces formed by the buildings where people can meet or sit and watch others (Whyte, 1980), and the interest at ground level – small shops, outdoor displays, or café life. These are all factors which people on foot rate as important, and help to contribute to the general well-being of the pedestrian.

## TRANSIT STREETS

These are streets where traffic has been removed and pavements widened to allow room for tree-planting, seats and bus shelters, with a minimum-width two-lane road for buses and trams, together with cycle lanes. The main pedestrian streets in the centre of Bremen have pavements removed, to allow paving to stretch the full width of the street, on which trams run. Where the street is wide enough this system works well, with tram lines making the pedestrian aware of possible danger. With bus-only streets this is more hazardous, although if the streets are well-landscaped they become more frequented by pedestrians. For example, when Philadelphia's Chestnut Street was surveyed, it was found that 64 per cent of pedestrians surveyed used the street more (UMTA, 1979).

## TRAFFIC CALMING

The second important contribution to walking in cities has been the introduction of 'traffic calming'. These are measures generally applied to residential areas, aimed at making streets safer to cross, by reducing vehicle speeds through minor alterations to the geometry of the road. Delft, in Holland, initiated a scheme experimentally in the early 1970s in an area of single-storeyed housing with a density of around 100 people to the hectare. The area was treated as basically a pedestrian zone, called a *Woonerf,* or town yard, where walking would be safe, and vehicles, although allowed in, would be slowed by providing humps, or by roads narrowed to 3 metres (10 feet) wide to slow their speed to walking pace. Parking requirements were low, so that space for planting, children's sandpits, or sitting out, could be set aside and the road bed paved over to provide an attractive walking environment. *Woonerfs* now exist in over 56 areas in Holland although they have proved expensive to build. They have since been adopted in Denmark and Germany in a simplified form called 'traffic calming'.

*Figure 34*  Delft, Holland. A traffic hump in part of the Woonerf or town yard scheme introduced in the 1970s to provide a safer environment for children to play in, and to walk within. Humps are now introduced in many countries as part of 'traffic calming' measures and are effective in reducing traffic speeds down to around 30 km/h (20 mph). Courtesy Van den Broek and Bakema.

*Figure 35*  View of a 'traffic calmed' street in Bruxtehude, a suburb of Hamburg where speeding on a long straight road has been reduced at junctions by narrowing the road just enough for two cars to pass slowly.

**Figure 36a** *Gothenburg, Sweden.*
*Traffic calming in residential area*
*adjoining the city centre.*
*Narrowing of two-way road to one lane*
*to reduce traffic speeds.*

**Figure 36b** *Narrowing and hump to*
*reduce speeds with side gaps in the*
*island for cyclists to pass and allow for*
*existing street drainage to be used*
*without being altered.*
Photos Ekman. Courtesy Goteborgs
Byggnadskontor.

*Figure 37*  *Careful detail on the main street in Bruxtehude at a pedestrian crossing to protect the tree. The crossing is paved in a different colour to the road surface.*

*Figure 38*  *Street junction in Kensington, London. The continuity of the main road is obtained through a slight hump which slows vehicles, and different-coloured paving demarcates the section as the pedestrian's domain, thus avoiding the legislation required to turn it into a zebra crossing.*
Courtesy Lousada.

These measures are implemented in streets, after careful consultation with residents where traffic volumes are low, around 250 vehicles per hour in both directions. A standard street sign is used, which designates the top speed at 30 km/h (20 mph) and schemes are generally carried out on an area-wide basis, closing some streets entering main roads to eliminate rat-running, with speed humps to reduce speeds. Road widths are often reduced to make it easier for pedestrians to cross to 5 metres (16 feet) wide for two-way and 3 metres (10 feet) for one-way traffic, and this has the effect of reducing vehicle speeds.

Traffic calming has benefited pedestrians, with estimates of accidents, by the German Federal Ministry of Transport, reduced to 5 per cent of their previous level. In North Rhine, Westphalia, 126 projects are being financed in 94 towns, at a cost of £53 million, with 25 per cent paid for by the local authorities, the remainder by Government (Hass-Klau, 1989). Costs of implementation are about the same as for ordinary roads – DM 90–105 per square metre (£22–£32 per square yard) – around half the cost of a pedestrian-only street.

## MAIN ROADS

Most main roads in cities already carry at peak hours a volume of traffic in excess of their environmental capacity. Sir Colin Buchanan in Traffic in Towns suggested that, among other solutions, one would be to build relief roads, taking traffic off the main roads, particularly where this was a local shopping street, and so improve walking conditions by pavement widening. However, to do this on a large scale can be both costly, and in environmental terms, destructive. New construction and road widening work was undertaken after the war, in many cities, and still is. It may well take many years to complete, and often has disastrous results – usually because of the scale of the work, and particularly where the road geometry is unnecessarily elaborate. Weather protection is important and, when roads are widened, pavements should also be widened and arcades or canopies provided for weather protection. Protection from wind and rain can help encourage all-weather walking, particularly where cities have a wet climate. Pavements must allow space for tree planting, signs, bus shelters, newspaper kiosks and outdoor cafés, as well as providing for cycle lanes.

Large office buildings or rapid-transit stations require pavements proportionately wider in front of their entrances to handle peak flows of

*Figure 39* Dropped kerbs at street junctions are among the first and most useful measures taken by authorities to improve walking conditions for disabled people and mothers with push chairs. Courtesy Tizard.

people. Additional space is also required at street junctions. In New York and other dense cities laid out on a regular grid, large volumes of office workers arrive almost simultaneously at light-controlled junctions, and can be forced on to the roads because of inadequate pavement space (Pushkarev and Zupan, 1975).

## ACCIDENTS

Street junctions and crossings remain the most critical points, where most pedestrian accidents take place. In 1985 in Britain 1787 pedestrians were killed and 58,500 injured – a high proportion being children. Outside the city centre a safe walk to school or to shops is important, and within residential areas, humps in the road will reduce traffic speeds and accidents. Along main roads on-street parking can be reduced, or eliminated, to allow pavement widening and tree planting and reduce the hazard from pedestrians stepping out between cars. In Britain stringent rules exist, which only allow zebra crossings to be located where pedestrian flows are double traffic flows. For them to be light-controlled requires pedestrian flows to be five times heavier. Far more crossings are, in fact, required, although this will mean a reduction in traffic flow. There is no reason why a pedestrian's time is not as valuable as a motorist's. No research is ever made to find out if pedestrians are taking alternative routes to cross a busy road with no crossing, or simply not making the trip on foot. A good level of street lighting helps to make walking safer, particularly where few people are about. Continuity of pavement surface is also important, along main roads, reducing the number of junctions, or narrowing them. Crossings

*Figure 40* View of a pedestrian subway at Altona, Hamburg, an interchange between bus and rail. Subways in German cities are frequently provided in redeveloped areas at an appropriate scale, planned as part of the overall environment. Well-lit and finished, they often have shops when connected to underground stations.

*Figure 41* Pedestrian conveyors at an H-Bahn station, Hanover. More easily used by mothers with push-chairs than escalators, disabled people still find them difficult to use.

**Figure 42**  Pedestrian bridge in Hamburg across the inner ring road linking with Dammtor station. Escalators and stairs are used to change level and the bridge is one of two linked through a small shopping arcade on the first floor of an existing building.

for main roads, apart from normal ground-level crossings may, on exceptionally busy roads, need to be underground, which in German city centres are models of what can and should be done. These often combine shops with an underground station and provide escalators or conveyors for the upward climb. Bridges, with ramps or escalators at each end, are only valid in exceptional situations where large roads must be crossed, usually outside the central area, or in exceptional situations within, as part of an elevated network.

## SEGREGATION

Ground-level walkways, usually in new residential areas, are frequently planned away from roads, to allow children to walk to a kindergarten, local shop, or playspace, without crossing traffic. Over short distances these have merit, although pedestrians can be vulnerable at night, and such walkways are often disliked for this reason. The traditional pavement bordering a road has the advantage of being more populated, and is preferable, while the recent North American policy of building housing estates with no pavements (sidewalks), is rapidly gaining favour in Europe, but is only valid when the roads are designed to be 'shared spaces' with humps to slow vehicle speeds.

## UNDERGROUND STREETS

The need for weather protection, in cities with extreme climates, has led Toronto and Montreal, following the construction of new underground railways, to develop underground pedestrian shopping streets, called in Toronto 'pathways', linking the stations with other development. Toronto now has 10 km (6.3 miles) of weather-protected 'pathways', privately financed and connecting three hotels, thirty offices, around a thousand shops and restaurants with five underground stations. Twenty parking garages are also linked to the network and the 'pathways' are a financial success and well-used by the public. Their principal shortcoming, apart from being underground and artificially lit, is that they are, like shopping malls, not truly a public space, available for use 24 hours a day, but are closed after office hours, although access to the stations from street level is still possible. The 'Pathway' system does, however, provide a useful facility for walking across the city centre, in extreme winter conditions.

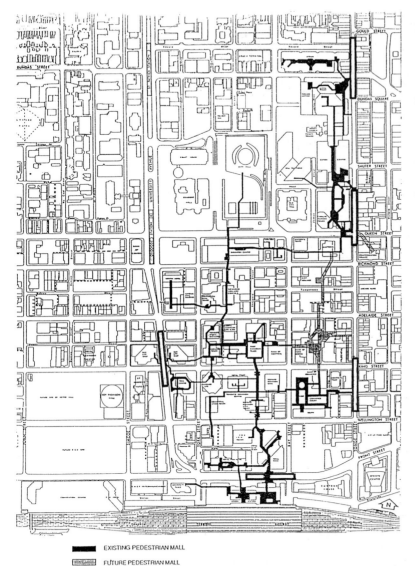

**Figures 43, 44** *Toronto's underground pedestrian mall walkway has developed as an extension of the underground railway and links its five stations through over 10 km (6 miles) of weather-protected shopping arcades. The network provides ideal walking conditions through the day in winter weather, less so on fine days and is closed at night, except for access points to the underground stations.*
Courtesy Toronto City Planning and Development Department.

EXISTING PEDESTRIAN MALL

FUTURE PEDESTRIAN MALL

INTERNAL SURFACE CONNECTION

SUBWAY STATION

## ELEVATED WALKWAYS

There has been, in thirteen 'winter cities' in North America, an alternative strategy for pedestrians, which uses elevated pedestrian walkways running through the centre of each city block, connected by means of bridges across the streets. Minneapolis started building these in 1962 and now has fourteen city blocks, linked at first- or second-floor levels, by glazed bridges. Called 'skyways', they have stair and escalator access down to street level at each bridge. Guidelines, set out by the city planning authority, require developers to provide a clear walking path 3.6 metres (12 feet) wide, with 2.4 metres (8 feet) headroom, and for them to be air-conditioned. Within existing buildings, small shops have been located along the walkways, replacing offices. Pedestrian counts showed that 96 per cent of pedestrians interviewed preferred using the skyways on a cold day (20°F or -7°C), compared to 71.7 per cent on average days (50–80°F or 10–20°C). Two factors are important:

1 'Skywalks' have limited opening hours, and like Toronto's 'pathways' are not open all night.
2 They tend to serve, because of the high office content and number of luxury shops, a high-income user, rather than people with modest incomes (Robertson, 1988).

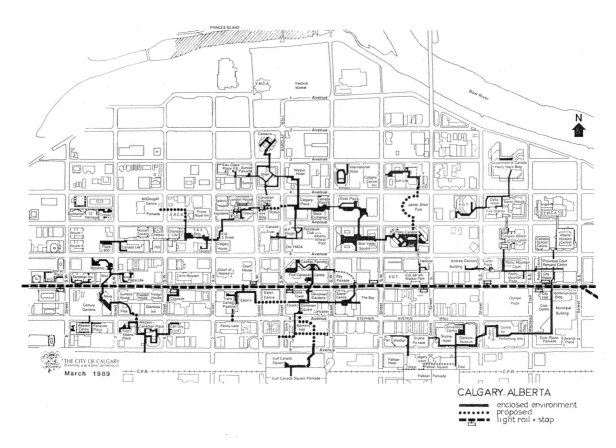

CALGARY. ALBERTA

━━━━━  enclosed environment
●●●●●●●  proposed
▬▬▬▬  light rail + stop

The effect on shopping at pavement level has been considerable, with ground-level pavements less well-used, except by the more socially disadvantaged.

Calgary, Alberta, a 'winter city' with a population of 650,000 people, rebuilt a large section of its city centre in the 1970s, using an elevated walkway system – over 9 km (5 miles) long, mostly climate-controlled, with 41 bridges crossing the street grid below, including light rail and bus system. Free travel is provided on the light rail, across the city centre, used by some 20,000 people daily, and around 22,000 parking spaces, out of 41,000, are connected directly to the walkway system, used by an estimated 19,000 pedestrians on weekdays. Some 45 per cent of work trips to the central area are made on public transport.

Much of the criticism of walkway systems, above or below ground, focuses on their 'sameness' and lack of variety or richness, and there

*Figure 45* Calgary, Alberta. Plan showing routes of over 8 km (5 miles) of elevated walkways mostly climate-controlled with 41 bridges crossing the existing street grid below. Around 45 per cent of work trips are made to the Central Area by bus or light rail, mostly on the transit mall indicated.

*Figure 46* Light-rail boarding platforms, elevated with ramped access for disabled people. Total enclosure of the platforms would have been an advantage to deal with the winter weather and integration of the stations into the bridges above. The light-rail system provides free travel for passengers within the central area.
Courtesy City of Calgary

*Figure 47* A typical bridge connecting two blocks over 7th Avenue. Many walkways are fully air-conditioned, affording total climate control in hot summers and sub-zero winters. They were built by private developers and taken over subsequently by the city as public spaces.
Courtesy City of Calgary

is a genuine need to provide for the small shopkeeper, with small kiosks, or market stalls, all of which tend to be sanitised or priced away, in the interests of hygiene, or because of fire regulations or unaffordable rents. Really to contribute to walking in cities and make them interesting, walkways have to rid themselves of the 'mall' image, generally aimed at higher-income social groups, and be permanently open, with some supervision, as well as be under the control, as in Calgary, of the city authority.

Clearly, in appalling weather conditions, they have advantages, and do not need to come to terms with problems of traffic or servicing. However, a ground-level solution does seem equally possible and one that could lead to a greater variety, at less cost. Street-level arcades could be used, wide – as in Bologna – radiant-heated, lined with small shops and kiosks and combined with streets closed to traffic and covered. Such networks have been created in some Japanese towns and are an environment which can be more easily changed and is readily accessible by public transport.

## WALKING AND TRANSPORT

The use of public transport generally involves a longer walking trip than one using the private car, and for this reason it is essential that the 'walking environment' is seen as an extension of the public transport system. For example 71 per cent of people using the London Underground walk to the station. Pedestrian areas have been very successful in extending the distance people will walk from public transport, once the conflict with vehicular traffic is removed.

Far too often transport planners are more concerned with the operation of their system, with journey speeds, and with reliability, than with the question of how convenient and accessible the system is for the pedestrian. It needs to be considered whether a system within a Central Area is better placed underground, with stations necessarily spaced widely apart, owing to their high cost, or, as in the case of light rail, for it to run at ground level, with stops close together, at low cost.

For public transport in future cities to be an acceptable alternative to the private car, walking conditions have to be improved and reconsidered.

# 3
# MOBILITY FOR ELDERLY AND DISABLED PEOPLE

In the UK there are an estimated 6 million people with some degree of disability, some 35 million in the United States and 42 million in Western Europe. In most countries, around 10–12 per cent of the population have some disability which gives them reduced mobility and 75 per cent of these are elderly.

There is an increasing effort being made to provide better transport for this growing sector of the population. To be mobile, and self-sufficient, is a high priority for elderly and disabled people, since this improves their well-being and reduces the cost of medical aid. In urban areas, these people are offered special transport facilities. On average, in the UK, only 10 per cent of the trips by elderly and disabled people on special services are work or medical trips, and leisure or shopping trips are more important (Oxley, 1988). This chapter identifies some of the approaches that are being made to the problem.

## WALKING

Elderly and ambulant disabled people would enjoy moving around freely in cities as much as the rest of the population were it not for being actually apprehensive. For them the quality of 'detail' of the overall network of pavements that they use is important. Pavement finishes have to be well drained and even, and free from parked cars. Street crossings, ideally, should be light controlled, with lights that 'talk' to help people with visual impairments (go: 'pip-pip') when traffic is halted. Dropped kerbs are required at junctions, ramped down to road level – to help people in wheelchairs who have difficulty stepping on and off kerbs, and studded paving across the pavement for blind people more easily to identify when a street crossing has been reached. Pavements ideally should be raised across secondary road junctions, to give continuity of surface. In many countries all new buildings have now, by law, to provide access for wheelchair users – with shallow ramps, wide doors and lifts to serve all floors. Many existing buildings too are being similarly adapted.

Pedestrian-only areas, if they are properly designed, can be a boon to the elderly and disabled people. With an increasingly aged population there is a strong case for providing more of them,

*Figure 48* Wheelchair user in pedestrian area, Essen. The pedestrian area is served by lift from bus and H-Bahn stations below and is well-used by unaccompanied wheelchair users who can cross the surrounding ring road by bridge from the adjoining residential areas.

particularly in shopping areas. But they must be easy to reach by public transport and provide adjacent parking for cars used by disabled people. Seats should be provided, well-placed, adjacent to, but not in, the flow of pedestrian traffic, with rest places alongside where wheelchair users can stop and rest. Shallow ramped underpasses are often carefully planned in German cities, below ring roads, and some use pedestrian conveyors for the upward climb rather than escalators, although conveyors cannot be used by people who are unsteady on their feet.

This attention to detail, applied to a central area, must similarly be applied throughout residential areas. Here, 'environmental area' planning should have eliminated through-traffic and 'traffic calming' (see Walking), using road humps, will have so slowed traffic that streets can be safely crossed, making it easier to make trips to local shops or to reach a bus stop (US DOT, 1980).

## PUBLIC TRANSPORT

It is important to provide 'user-friendly' transport systems best suited to the local needs of the elderly and disabled. They should have their own representatives on any transport advisory committee. Regular dispersal of accurate information, on new or available services, is required. Drivers must be trained to understand their problems. The delay at a bus or tram stop caused by disabled people boarding has been shown by research to be exaggerated, making no measurable delay in running time.

### Dial-a-ride

This is a bus, often radio controlled, developed in the 1960s as a public transport system, which in recent years has tended to be run as a service for disabled people (ECMT, 1987). Easy access to a phone is important, as is the ease with which the booking is made. Usually regular passengers have a code number, giving their address, which identifies them, and this and the required destination are often typed into a small computer which identifies a suitable vehicle. The passenger is then informed when the pick-up will take place. Two operations are normal: the 'many to many' trip which offers an unlimited choice of destinations, but uses up valuable vehicle time, or the 'many to few' trip where a set number of destinations are provided, allowing more people to use the system. The vehicles are ideally specially adapted minibuses, with a lift or ramp at the rear, or side space for typically two wheelchairs, and low boarding steps with special hand-holds. Dial-a-ride can be expensive to operate. In London, estimated costs are between £8 and £16 per trip and an annual government subsidy of £7 million is provided (Oxley, 1988). Elsewhere the services can be provided much more cheaply at £2–£3 per trip.

### Taxis

Some authorities prefer to use taxis, which may be only marginally more costly or may cost less than dial-a-ride. London's new taxicabs, the Metrocab and the Fairway, cost around £15,000, have high, wide doors, opening 90°, with a low floor for easy boarding by wheelchair users. Detachable ramps are provided, for boarding from road level, with special driver-controlled anchoring for wheelchairs, and space for four passengers. There is now a statutory requirement for all new London taxis to be wheelchair accessible. Most authorities in London

*Figure 49* Wheelchair passenger using a demountable ramp fitted to a 'Fairway' taxi. Automatic floor-holding fastenings, operated by the driver keep the wheelchair static. All new London taxis must now provide access for wheelchair users. Many provide a service for disabled people who are issued with vouchers by the local authorities. Courtesy London Taxis International.

provide a Taxicard scheme to subsidise the fare. The passenger pays the first £1, then the local authority pays up to £7 – 60 per cent of the fare on the meter. In some cities, taxis are extensively used by old people. In Berlin, for example, in a 1979 study, 25 per cent of taxi users were over 65 years old. In Hanover, the drivers on the light railway will, on request, telephone ahead for a taxi to meet a passenger at a suburban stop.

## Buses

Bus operators approach the problems of dealing with wheelchair passengers in different ways. In Halmstad, Sweden, 50 raised bus stops, approached by ramp, have been built, out of a total of 400 stops in the town. Special Volvo buses are used, with automatically extending bridges to span the gap at door entry-points. This has been in operation for ten years, successfully, although it has created problems in severe winter weather. In recent years in the United States, all new buses purchased with Federal funds have had to be provided with wheelchair lifts, although this requirement is now being relaxed. Elsewhere, operators question the necessity of providing this expensive facility, if stops are difficult to reach. Generally, European operators are ordering better designed standard buses, with low-

**Figure 50** *Low-loading buses fitted with driver-controlled extendable ramps and wide doors providing access from the kerb for wheelchair passengers. Alternative and more elaborate solutions tried in Sweden require high-level platforms to suit the vehicle rather than redesign it, as has been done here.* Courtesy Neoplan.

**Figure 52** *The Airbus service running from central London to Heathrow airport has a lift for wheelchair passengers. The Carelink service interchanges with Airbus and provides a service to all mainline stations, allowing wheelchair users arriving by rail to reach the airport unaccompanied. With around 10 per cent of the population disabled in most countries and a growing sector of the population elderly, there is good reason for urban transport systems to be planned to provide an adequate service.* Courtesy London Regional Transport.

boarding steps, and conveniently placed, often textured, and colour-contrasted hand-holds, aimed at serving ambulant disabled and elderly people. Special services are then run which provide access for wheelchair passengers. For example, London Regional Transport runs a Mobility Bus on several set routes, once a day, with lift and space for up to five wheelchair passengers, to local shopping centres, returning after one-and-a-half hours on the same route. The 'Airbus' fleet running from Central London, stops at Heathrow Airport at 20-minute intervals. All buses have lifts and interchange with the 'Carelink' shuttle service. This links the main line stations and long-distance train services carrying wheelchair passengers by prior arrangement.

## Light rail
New light-rail cars, such as are used in Grenoble, have a central car with a floor 34 cm (13½ inches) high and these low-loading cars are preferable to the fold-down steps used elsewhere. In some cities, as in Calgary, Alberta, raised platforms are used in the central area, and are approached by ramp, and although these are visually obstructive, they do make the system accessible for wheelchair users.

London's Dockland Light Railway has all its platforms raised to the same level as the car floor, although a gap of about 75 mm (3 inches) has to be negotiated. Platform edges are in white grooved precast concrete, and hydraulic lifts are provided to all platforms, from street level. In Newcastle's Tyne and Wear metro, although used by an average of nine wheelchair users daily, the lifts at all stations are used by many ambulant and disabled people and people with prams and shopping trolleys. An estimated £6 million was spent in providing for disabled people.

## Rapid transit
All new rapid-transit systems being built in Europe and North America provide access by lift from street to platform level, with special details, coloured handrails, etc. to suit ambulant disabled people. In Stockholm specially built enclosed stair lifts, similar to domestic ones, are provided at some stations, running parallel with the escalator. This is in direct contrast to such expensively built new systems as are found in Hong Kong and Singapore, where little provision for disabled people is made (Heraty, 1989).

In existing underground railways, such as those in London, because of the prohibitive cost, lifts cannot generally be provided to all stations, although 18 existing ones are being evaluated and new stations will

**Figure 51** *Docklands Light Railway in London has precast, ribbed, non-slip and easily identifiable, concrete edges to all platforms for disabled people. Vehicle floors are the same level as platforms for the benefit of wheelchair-users, who use hydraulic lifts to reach all platforms.*
Courtesy London Regional Transport

have lifts. The approach adopted is rather to provide appropriate details when a station is refurbished to better suit the needs of ambulant disabled people.

## CARS

In the UK, there are an estimated 200,000 disabled drivers, in Germany, 1.2 million, who can drive specially adapted cars (Oxley, 1988). The adaptation of the car is either paid for privately or many European countries fund car provision including the cost of adaptations. In the United States, if the driver is a war veteran, a government grant is made. In Germany, support is only given if the driver is unable to use public transport, and permanently dependent on the use of a car to reach a place of work or rehabilitation centre (ECMT, 1988). Cars used by disabled people display a badge, usually allowing them special parking concessions. Specially wide and signposted parking bays are required, ideally 3.9 metres (13 feet) wide, located close to pedestrian areas or station entrances. There is a strong case for encouraging disabled people to drive, if they can afford to, and so widen their choice of workplace.

This brief survey shows how urban transport is being planned, designed and adapted in many countries, to serve a growing demand for mobility by elderly and disabled people. It is always cheaper and easier to 'build in' than to 'bolt on' and planners and operators are becoming more aware that elderly and disabled people are an increasingly large segment of public transport users and cannot be any longer dismissed as a 'difficult minority'.

# 4
# CYCLING

Cycling in cities is now seen by transport planners as a means of transport worthy of consideration. There is a strong case for encouraging cycling as a non-polluting form of transport, which can be enjoyable, useful and cheap to use. Generally in cities of up to 250,000 people, if the topography is flat, more people cycle because distances are short. There is less traffic congestion and it is here that special provision for cycling is made. How much people cycle will depend on a number of factors:

1   Topography. A hilly terrain will deter cyclists, with around 50 per cent more cycling in flat country. In Holland and Denmark 40 per cent of people use cycles more than any other form of transport, while only 7 per cent in Britain use a cycle more than once a week.
2   Adverse weather deters even the most ardent cyclist – especially snow and ice.
3   Safety conditions will for many people decide if the trip is made by cycle or not. Children are particularly at risk, with accidents in the UK to the under-10s more likely than for any other age group, with 20,000–24,000 accidents each year, 300 of them fatal, and most occurring at junctions, in collisions with vehicles.
4   Speed and convenience. Cycles are cheap to buy and maintain and are widely used if time is saved on the journey to work. Cycling is four times faster than walking, but cyclists, like pedestrians, will rarely deviate more than 10 per cent off the direct route.
5   Space. Cyclists take up under half the space of a car, in movement, but only one-twentieth of the space of a car, when parked. In cities where no cycle tracks are provided cycling numbers are low. However, in Copenhagen since the introduction of cycle lanes, beside all main roads, cycling has doubled, and 9 per cent of work trips to the centre are now made by cycle. Only in China does the density of cyclists exceed that of vehicles, with one intersection in Beijing used by over 10,000 cycles in one hour (Jun Meng Yang, 1985). In Erlangen, West Germany, with a population of 103,000, following cycle improvement schemes, introduced by the Mayor for political reasons, cycling has doubled in five years, with car use reduced by an estimated 10 per cent.

**Figure 53** Copenhagen, Denmark. Cycle tracks are provided alongside almost every main road in the city centre – a total of around 30 km (18 miles) of track. Since their introduction around 10–20 per cent of people journey to work in the centre, an increase of 6000 in the last five years, and this represents one third of all trips previously made by car into the centre.

**Figure 54** *Cycle track in Bruxtehude,
near Hamburg. German towns and cities
frequently provide cycle tracks, finished
in a different colour, beside the
pavement.*

## CYCLING PROVISION

There are many improvements to roads being steadily implemented to help cyclists, but few examples exist, with the exception of Copenhagen, where provision for cycling has meant a reduction of road space. Unlike walking, cycling is, however, seen by some politicians as a 'green' form of transport which is non-polluting and requires no subsidy, once cycle lanes are in place.On main roads there is a range of measures which can provide for better cycling conditions:

1   Bus lanes. These may be shared with cyclists, but are not ideal, as buses travel at about the same speed and require that a cyclist stops when the bus stops. To combine bus lanes with freight traffic (see Freight) would make the problem worse.

2   A painted line on the road following the kerb and 2–2.5 metres (6–8 feet) from it will demark space for up to 1000 cycles per hour

*Figure 55* Cycle parking at Niendorf-Markt interchange station, Hamburg, serving the S-Bahn station below. Cycle parking is an important part of many transport systems and allows easy, inexpensive access to and from home to stations or bus stops although parking should still be provided. In Japan an estimated 1.25 million cycles are daily parked at railway stations.

(Hudson, 1982). To be effective this requires that roads are free of parked cars and delivery vehicles. Wide pedestrian pavements in Hamburg are part paved in a different colour and used as cycle tracks in the central area.

3  Segregated cycle lanes may be possible, in special cases, and are usually found either in new towns, or smaller towns, where space permits and traffic flows are low.

4  Contra-flow lanes may be provided to overcome the problems caused to cyclists on one-way streets. This will be either a marked section of the road, with special provision at the entry and exit points, or if space permits a 1.5–2 metre (5–6 foot) wide lane separated from the road by a narrow raised strip.

5  Various designs of junctions provide a turning lane for cyclists to cross oncoming traffic, and are light-controlled.

6  Within pedestrian-only areas in many European cities cycling is permitted, although questionable, where large numbers are involved because of the risk to pedestrians.

7  Signposted routes for cycling, or non-cycling, are important, and designated cycle routes need to be made legal. At present no universally recognised sign system exists for cycling (Hudson, 1982).


## PARKING

Cycles normally require the provision of objects to which they can be locked on the street, as theft is universal, except in China, where cycles are licensed. As the number of cycles increases, so parking becomes more space-consuming (Grabe and Utech, 1984), particularly around public transport facilities. In Japan, an estimated 1.25 million cycles are daily parked at railway stations, occasionally underground, or, in one case, in a multi-storeyed car park. In The Netherlands an estimated 90,000 covered and guarded cycle parking spaces are provided at 80 of the principal stations, with the railway providing the space, and charging a fee, which covers about three-quarters of the cost (Replogle, 1983). In California, lockers are provided at some bus stations, and the Dutch principle of providing guarded parking at stations is normal. Developers should be obliged to provide cycle parking space in all new city development projects. In addition, all pedestrian areas require adjacent cycle parks, preferably at their perimeter.

## POSTSCRIPT

One of the most interesting experiments in cycling in recent years was introduced in Amsterdam by a radical student group, the Provos. In an effort to combat increasing traffic congestion, white painted cycles were left in groups around the central area, intended to be picked up and left as required. Many were either stolen or ended up in the canals. However, today free white bicycles are used and enjoyed by visitors to the park of the Kroller Muller Museum outside Amsterdam.

**Figure 56** *Four hundred white cycles are provided at the National Park, Otterloo, near Amsterdam, Holland. These are free for the use of visitors to the park.*
*White cycles were introduced by a radical student group in Amsterdam in the 1970s, who thought that they would be a way of reducing increasing congestion in the centre.*
Courtesy Margaret Macdonald.

# 5
# THE CAR

Cars, for many people who own one, are the most useful means of transport available. They represent a high capital investment. Once purchased, they frequently result in their drivers making more trips a day than they did before owning one – trips which need no longer rely on public transport. Car ownership is increasing in all cities, except where either parking costs are high, or where there is no economic restraint through high taxation. In Manhattan, for example, few people keep cars, because of parking problems, and in Singapore fewer cars are being purchased, because of high import duties. Car ownership is significantly higher in the United States, with one car per 1.7 persons on average, compared with Europe's one car per 2.9 persons (excluding Portugal and Greece). Two-car family ownership continues to rise in all countries (National Travel Survey, 1988). However, around 30 per cent of the population, in all countries, is either too young, or too old, to drive.

Cars used at peak periods seriously congest essential traffic in all cities, principally buses and service vehicles, unless bus-only lanes are provided, and new road-building in cities will not satisfy the demand for space at peak periods, unless measures of restraint on car use are imposed. President Pompidou's advice on road-building, *Il faut adapter Paris aux automobiles* ('It is necessary to adapt Paris for use by cars'), was fortunately only partially carried out. It did, however, destroy, for pedestrian use, the banks of the River Seine, in the centre of Paris. Even in low-density cities such as Los Angeles with over 200 km (125 miles) of freeway, started in 1941, it is now accepted that more freeway construction cannot keep up with demand. The future lies in encouraging drivers on to improved systems of public transport, and for them to use cars in innovative ways, such as car-sharing.

Constraints on driving cars into city centres occur when congestion reaches a level where drivers will transfer on to rail (Mogridge, 1985), provided it is more convenient, and quicker than driving. Some restraints are imposed on cars in central areas through parking controls, although, as discussed later, these are not very effective (May, 1986). In addition, company cars whose drivers commute, estimated in London to be 30 per cent of cars (TEST, 1984), are, in part, tax deductible, and so are subsidised directly. This is at odds with any policy aimed at freeing roads for bus operation.

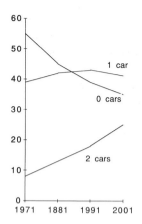
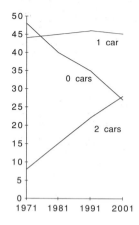

**Figures 57, 58**  *The diagrams show the steady growth of two-car ownership in the UK (as a percentage of households), like many other countries.*
Source National Travel Survey.

**Figure 59**  *Vehicle use in selected countries in the world, showing the number of vehicles (in thousands)  and the average number of people per vehicle.*

| Country | Cars | Persons per car | Commercial vehicles | Total vehicles | Persons per vehicle |
|---|---|---|---|---|---|
| *EEC* | | | | | |
| Belgium | 3 498 | 2.8 | 383 | 3 880 | 2.6 |
| Denmark | 1 588 | 3.2 | 295 | 1 882 | 2.7 |
| France | 21 970 | 2.5 | 4 223 | 26 193 | 2.1 |
| Germany West | 28 304 | 2.2 | 1 814 | 30 118 | 2.0 |
| Greece | 1 379 | 7.2 | 627 | 2 006 | 5.0 |
| Irish Republic | 737 | 4.8 | 110 | 856 | 4.1 |
| Italy | 22 500 | 2.5 | 1 897 | 24 397 | 2.3 |
| Luxembourg | 162 | 2.3 | 15 | 177 | 2.1 |
| Netherlands | 5 118 | 2.8 | 506 | 5 624 | 2.6 |
| Portugal | 1 290 | 7.9 | 394 | 1 684 | 6.1 |
| Spain | 9 750 | 4.0 | 1 750 | 11 500 | 3.4 |
| United Kingdom | 20 606 | 2.7 | 2 915 | 23 521 | 2.4 |
| | | | | | |
| Norway | 1 623 | 2.6 | 303 | 1 926 | 2.2 |
| Sweden | 3 367 | 2.5 | 260 | 3 626 | 2.3 |
| Switzerland | 2 733 | 2.3 | 229 | 2 961 | 2.2 |
| | | | | | |
| Canada | 11 477 | 2.2 | 3 212 | 14 689 | 1.7 |
| | | | | | |
| Japan | 29 478 | 4.1 | 20 424 | 49 901 | 2.4 |
| | | | | | |
| USA | 139 041 | 1.7 | 41 948 | 180 989 | 1.3 |

**Figure 60**  *Right bank of the River Seine, Paris, abandoned as a calm area for walking and from which to fish in favour of a two-lane road – part of President Pompidou's doctrine of trying to adapt Paris to the automobile, and succeeding only in bringing more traffic into the centre.*
Courtesy Lousada.

## PARKING

Two types of parking are available in cities – private and public. At present restraint on cars entering a central area can only be exercised by controls on public car parks, or on-street parking through pricing. Neither is effective.

### Private car parks

These have been over-provided in the past, in new developments, and this has meant that large numbers of car commuters enjoy free parking during the day. London has now reduced the parking provision for offices to one space per 1100 square metres (12,000 square feet). Munich allows developers to contribute funds towards building public car spaces, rather than below their own buildings. All private car parks, ideally, should be used for short-term use, and opened after the

*Figure 61* Parking space in residential areas is now often fully saturated, with a shortage of off-street parking. One solution, adopted in Japanese towns, is to require all car owners to provide off-street parking. Alternatively this could be required for households with two cars. Courtesy Lousada.

morning peak, but to do this is politically difficult. One solution would be to change the present rating system according to the number of spaces provided, or to levy a special tax on the parking provided (Plowden, 1980).

### Public car parks

These should be priced at an economic rent, and be available only for short-term use. They continue to be built in some cities for political reasons by authorities, who heavily subsidise their construction. Many are badly sited in central areas, where the necessary access roads conflict with expanding pedestrian areas. The City of York is now considering closure of some parking for this reason.

### On-street parking

There is much on-street parking within central areas which could usefully be removed for environmental reasons and so allow for pavements to be widened and trees to be planted.

### Residents' parking

Normally, new housing development requires off-street parking provision at one car space per unit plus a shared provision for visitors. All Japanese towns require off-street parking to be provided for every car owner. On-street residents' parking, throughout a city, must ultimately be licensed, to prevent the use of road-space for commuters' cars.

### Park-and-ride

This is an important way of keeping cars to the periphery of cities, but unless housed in multi-storeyed parks uses up valuable land. Ideally, it could usefully serve short-term parkers, such as shoppers, who would be charged at an economic rate (see Interchanges).

### CAR-POOLING

This became widespread in North America in the 1970 fuel crisis, and is continually encouraged by authorities there, keen to reduce congestion and single-car occupancy by commuters. Car-pooling normally involves employees who live and work in the same area, work the same hours and organise themselves, or have it done for them, by an organisation. In Pleasanton, California, for example, local planning requirements have so encouraged car-pooling, that single-car occupancy at peak hours has been reduced by 36 per cent (Orski, 1988). In Singapore, stops are provided for car-poolers, near bus stops in the suburbs, and cars carrying three or more passengers are allowed through the cordon area free of charge. Of around 16,000 cars studied entering during the morning peak over half were car-poolers. However, only 10 per cent of car-poolers share a car on the return trip (World Bank, 1984).

## TAXIS

These are an essential part of a city transport system, providing a personal service equivalent to the private car, without the necessity of owning one. Taxis in the United States carry a significant proportion of travellers, with an estimated 40 per cent more passengers using them than all the rapid transit systems combined. Fares are, however, around three times more per passenger trip, and five times more per passenger mile, than for public transport (Wohl, 1976). In New York, in spite of restrictive licensing regulations, around one million people use cabs daily. In Washington DC an estimated 100,000 people use taxis daily – one third of the bus patronage.

Taxis are allowed to use bus lanes in some cities, which on busy routes is questionable, because when stopped they block the buses behind. Taxi ranks are an important facility, and can mean that cruising for hire, which adds to road congestion, can be banned. Ranks should be located close to Metro entrances, as in Paris, and equipped with phones. Radio control for taxis is invaluable. Although expensive, it allows a taxi to be called and provide door-to-door service – a boon for old people (see Mobility for elderly and disabled people). It can also provide valuable help to emergency services – fire, police, or ambulance – in the event of a roadside accident. In Copenhagen, all taxis must have radios, while in London only 5000 out of 15,000 licensed taxis have them. The cost of manpower at a central control room has now been reduced through a Canadian development using computerised dispatching. One radio taxi company, 'Dial-a-Cab', has recently installed such a system for its 1400 cabs in London, costing £2.5 million. This will use fewer radio channels and handle 42,000 jobs daily instead of 6000.

The licensing of taxicabs, while adding to the cost of a fare, ensures the passenger a degree of security and safety. In London licensed taxis are tested annually for roadworthiness, and are specially robust diesel-powered vehicles costing over £15,000 each, with an average seven-year life. New vehicles are obliged to be provided with a ramp for the disabled. All are metered, with a fare structure set by the licensing authority, and the equipment is regularly checked for faults.

## CAR HIRE

In London, in addition to licensed taxis, an estimated 20,000 minicabs operate – mostly outside the central area – run by small private operators, usually one-man firms, using their own standard cars with short-wave radios. Tariffs are by negotiation, as they have no meters. The cars are forbidden by law to ply for hire and future legislation will shortly require them all to be registered.

## JITNEYS

Jitneys are shared taxis. They began operation in the United States around 1915, when an estimated 62,000 were running, driver-owned Ford Model T's, which cruised the streets picking up passengers from bus stops, at a flat fare of 5 cents. It was estimated that around half the number of streetcar passengers were being carried by jitneys in cities until the transport operators closed them down by 1920. Today jitneys run in low-income ghettos in New York and Pittsburgh, where public transport is poor, and provide a valuable, if illegal, service. Elsewhere in the world – notably Caracas, Mexico City, Tehran and Manila – jitneys also operate. Often small, open-sided, and brightly-painted transit vans accessible from the rear, they provide a useful service, although their large numbers frequently congest other traffic.

Today there is a case for allowing licensed jitneys to operate outside central areas, in low density areas, where public transport operators cannot run economic services. For example transit vans, painted in distinctive colours and privately owned could act as feeder systems to rapid transit stations. This could be agreed with the transport authority, who would require services to operate as well, outside the peak hours. Hanover has such a service, using shared taxi-vans from H-Bahn stations at night.

## MINICARS

The small inexpensive car is one which has been tried over the years and remains an untapped market. These vehicles are found in France, either battery-operated, or with 50cc engines and a length of 1.5–2

metres (5–6 feet 6 inches) allowing them to park at right angles to the kerb. Denmark has a similar electric car under development. Such cars take up half the parking space of a conventional car, can be non-polluting, if electric, and are useful for shopping or short trips.

Minicars were developed in the United States in 1969, sponsored by the Department of Transport. A car was developed with a hybrid engine, petrol, for use outside the centre, electric, for city use. The technology for hiring to key-holders was also developed, which recorded who had used the car, and billed the driver. A car-hire fleet, called the 'Witkar' or white car, was launched in Amsterdam in 1973, using two-person electric cars, which recharged themselves at terminals. Here the driver, who had a subscription and key, could pick up or leave the car. Witkar probably failed because only three terminals were built, but the idea could be applied to a public authority who needed its staff to make rapid visits to different parts of a city, and so avoid the need for a conventional car fleet or company car.

*Figure 62* Electric two-seater car manufactured by Whisper in Denmark. This is one of many attempts to produce a small, non-polluting vehicle suitable for short distance movement.
A fleet of vehicles such as these could be used by local authorities as an alternative to fleet cars, to visit sites etc., taking up less road space when parked or moving, or for use in lower density areas. Otherwise, unless all cars and other vehicles were of similar dimensions they offer no relief to present traffic conditions.

# 6

# ROAD-PRICING AND CONTROLS

The idea that drivers should pay for the privilege of driving on congested roads was first put forward in 1959 in Washington DC, and subsequently in London in 1964 by the Smeed Committee. These ideas came at a time when cities were equally congested, traffic speeds in London, as now, were around 19 km/h (12 mph), and suggested that road space was so valuable that it should be charged for or 'priced'. It was considered feasible that a device could be developed and attached to each car which would contain so many 'units' of use, purchased regularly and replaced when the 'units' were used up by passing over cables set in the road bed (Roth, 1967).

Such far-sighted proposals came at a time when even parking meters were not yet in use, and were regarded as unrealistic. Subsequent research into the feasibility of the proposals led to the development of the 'black box' by the Transport and Road Research Laboratory in 1968, the forerunner of the device used 15 years later in Hong Kong.

## ROAD-PRICING

In 1983, the first pilot scheme for road-pricing began in Hong Kong, where cable loops were laid out in the road bed at 18 sites and electronic number plates (ENP) were fitted to the underside of 2600 government cars on a test basis. Roadside outstations beside each cable loop, about the size of the boxes used beside traffic lights, transmitted a coded message back to the central computer. This identified which vehicle had passed over the cable, and at what time, and calculated the amount which each vehicle owner would be required to pay on a monthly basis. The ENP attached below each vehicle cost around £40 each, could be fitted in about seven minutes, and was a 'passive' system. Each electronic loop was easily laid, identical to those used at traffic lights, and the experiment proved to be 99 per cent reliable. The system was planned to cover the Central Area in a series of zones and be installed in three years. Charges in each zone would be set at a level to restrain vehicle trips at peak hours. An estimated rate of return on the investment of around 300 per cent was expected (Fong, 1985).

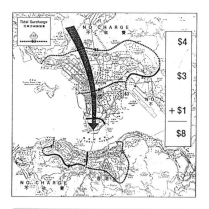

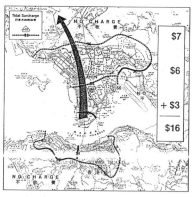

*Figure 63* Maps of central Hong Kong showing suggested cost of making a journey across the centre in the morning or evening peak hours and aimed at reducing peak-hour travel as a result. The Hong Kong road-pricing system was experimental and proved to be 99 per cent reliable but was not proceeded with, largely for political reasons and the degree of privacy drivers felt was lost through having to record where they were each day.

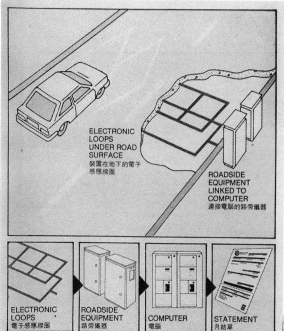

*Figures 64, 65* Diagram and photo of experimental road-pricing system tried in Hong Kong in 1983, showing how electronic loops are laid in the road bed and connected to roadside computers. Courtesy Hong Kong Secretary for Transport.

*Figure 66 (far left)* Roadside computers are connected to the central computer which identifies the number plates of the cars passing over the loop and records the time.

*Figure 67 (left)* Cars are fitted with passive boxes, costing around £40 each, which are welded to the underside of the chassis in around 10 minutes. Called an ENP or electronic number plate, this identifies the number plate of each car.

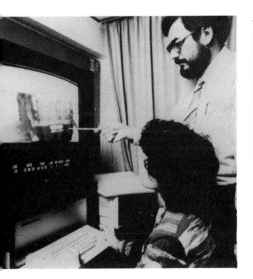

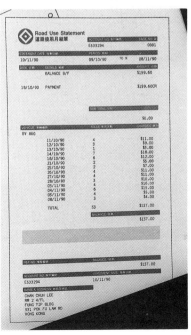

*Figure 68 (far left)* Any car without an ENP is automatically identified by video camera at the control centre and its road-license number plate recorded for later billing.

*Figure 69 (left)* Copy of a typical monthly bill sent to drivers identifying which zones have been passed through, stating the day, time and charge. Courtesy Hong Kong Secretary for Transport.

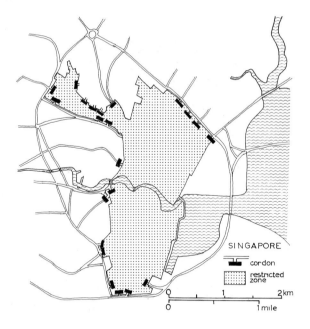

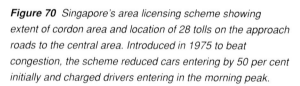

**Figure 70** *Singapore's area licensing scheme showing extent of cordon area and location of 28 tolls on the approach roads to the central area. Introduced in 1975 to beat congestion, the scheme reduced cars entering by 50 per cent initially and charged drivers entering in the morning peak.*

**Figure 71** *Daily or monthly licenses are purchased at booths off main roads, for display in side windows where they are visible to roadside police.*
Courtesy Armstrong-Wright

Unfortunately, local political factors resulted in the abandonment of the system. There were objections on the grounds of loss of privacy, because the system itemised the location of each vehicle, at each time of day, and also because the vehicle tax on cars in Hong Kong had just been raised (Borins, 1988). However, the experiment promoted wide interest and important lessons have been learnt.

## AREA LICENSING

In Singapore in 1975, because of growing congestion in the business district by 74,000 cars in the morning peak, an area licensing system was introduced, which required cars passing the 28 points of entry to display a pre-purchased licence. Today, this costs £1.50 (S$5) per day or £31 monthly (S$100), and is displayed in the top left-hand side of

**Figure 72** *Car-pool queue adjoining a bus stop outside the cordon area allows cars to pick up three passengers and drive in free of charge.*
Courtesy Armstrong-Wright.

**Figure 73** *Daily charges for licenses are around £1.50, with company cars charged at double the rate.*

the car windscreen, large enough to be seen by police officers at the control points. Should a vehicle not have a valid licence the number of the car is recorded manually, and a summons issued subsequently, with a £15 fine (S$50). Infringements are about 60 per day, and company cars are charged at double the rate, with taxis at under half the rate. Cars with three people and over (car-pools) and freight vehicles are allowed in free. The licensing system operates from 7.30 a.m. to 10.15 a.m., and with most shops opening after 10 a.m., the restrictions have no adverse effect on shopping. Business meetings tend to occur after 10am and while hotels situated outside the cordon area advertise that they are 'cordon-free', those inside do not appear to suffer (World Bank, 1984). Initially 90 additional buses were provided to serve special park-and-ride areas, just outside the cordon area, but these proved to be unpopular and they were closed. Bus services have been extended into residential areas, with commuters now using them for the entire trip, or the newly opened rapid-transit system.

Area licensing in Singapore has been estimated to reduce the entry by cars to about 50 per cent of what it might otherwise have been. Car traffic has, however, still grown, with many entering before 7.30 a.m. or, through increased affluence, prepared to pay the £31 (S$100) monthly licence fee. Moreover, the evening peak traffic leaving, when no controls exist, is about 100 per cent higher than the morning peak.

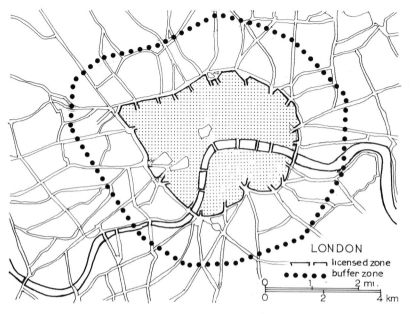

**Figure 74a** *Diagram showing an area licensing scheme for central London proposed in 1974 by the Greater London Council. As for Singapore, 200 signed entry-points would be required, manned by police, and licenses would have to be pre-purchased and displayed in car windows. The effects were estimated to reduce traffic by a third in the central area and by a tenth in the inner area.*

*An improved public transport system would be required and annual revenue of £45 million (at 1974 prices) partly put towards the cost of subsidising it. Sections of the inner ring road would have carried increased traffic and be improved, possibly by tunnelling.*
Courtesy Greater London Council.

In London an area licensing scheme was proposed by the Greater London Council in 1974 (GLC, 1974) and, as in Singapore, this proposed a cordon around the central area measuring about 3.4 km by 6.4 km (3 miles by 4 miles), bounded by the existing roads. Improvements would be made, on one section, to handle the predicted increase in traffic. Around 200 signed entry points were to be located around the cordon area and about 400 additional police were required to check the licensing, which would operate on weekdays only, between 8 a.m. and 6 p.m. Licences would be normally pre-bought at offices, or ticket machines. Cars, representing two out of every three vehicles entering the central area, would be licensed, as well as commercial vehicles and tourist coaches. Buses, taxis, motorcycles, emergency vehicles and cars for the disabled would not be licensed.

The traffic effects were calculated to result in a reduction of a third in the central area and a tenth in the inner area. This would allow enough spare road capacity to enable buses to run faster, and keep to time. The scheme would have required between 50 and 100 additional buses, and improvements to increase the capacity of the Underground. Fewer on-street parking meters would be required, and so environmental areas could be introduced, displacing the internal traffic on to the main roads. Private car parks were intended to be closed and

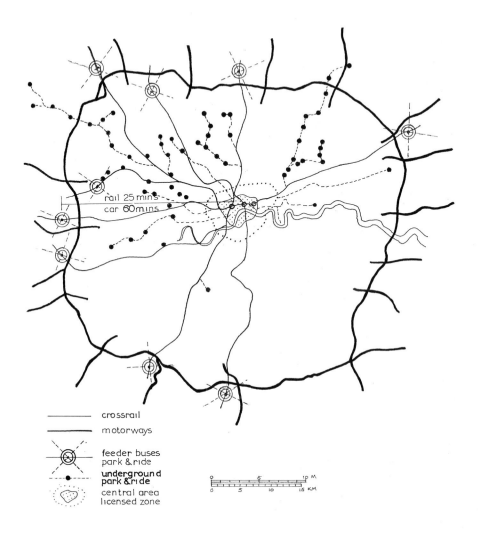

rail 25 mins
car 60 mins

———— crossrail
———— motorways
feeder buses
park & ride
**underground**
**park & ride**
central area
licensed zone

0    5    10 M
0    5    10    15 KM

**Figure 74b** *Plan showing suggested park-and-ride car parks located outside the M25 circular motorway, already overloaded in sections. Parking could be linked to the centre by Crossrail, an upgraded railway like the Métro Régional in Paris. Locations of existing car parks are also shown at underground stations, some of which could be double-decked, provided the surrounding roads had any spare capacity.*
Project Brian Richards.

used for other purposes. The scheme was at 1974 prices estimated to cost £5–8 million a year to operate, bringing in about £45 million a year in revenue, with a loss in fuel tax of around £10 million a year. The money gained would be available to subsidise public transport or for other needs in London.

Objections to the scheme were raised on the grounds of equity. The poor, unable to pay the licence fee, but needing a car in the centre for work purposes, would be unfairly taxed off the road. However, the benefits in terms of overall travel improvements for bus operation, plus the environmental improvements for those walking, negate these arguments. The GLC study proposed that all 60,000 private parking spaces would be taken over and today this would appear to be one problem requiring to be overcome, if area licensing for Central London were to be successful (LPAC, 1989).

## TOLL SYSTEMS

In the last three years there has been a rapid development in electronics by manufacturers in Europe and the United States working on 'smart card' technology for use by vehicles at toll gates. Alesund in Norway was the first town to use the Premid system developed by Philips, where an ID plate, the size of a large matchbox, is purchased by a regular commuter at his or her local bank and used as a weekly, monthly or annual permit to drive through a toll barrier. The plate is placed in the side window of the vehicle and read by one of three antennae units mounted on a pole by the roadside. The antennae emit microwaves at a very low power, reflected back from the ID plate, which, if up to date, turns a traffic light green, or, if out of date turns it red. The driver then either pays at the toll booth or the number plate is videoed automatically and the driver is sent a demand. The system has been operating satisfactorily 24 hours a day for two years and is used by 80 per cent of vehicles in the rush hour, at an average speed of 30 km/h (18 mph). It allows through up to 1500 vehicles an hour and the equipment for two lanes costs around £20,000. The device could be developed into a road licensing system, with a number of checkpoints provided across a central area, as well as at the periphery, and overcomes the 'privacy' criticism levelled at the Hong Kong system.

These developments in new technology could make road-pricing a reality, given the political will by governments to enforce them. Sweden is now studying the legal and technical problems, in depth, and a Research Board will eventually report back to their government.

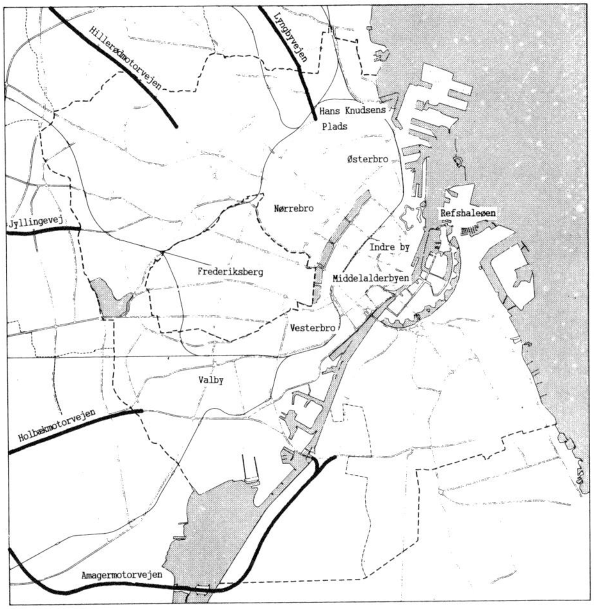

**Figure 75** *Map of Copenhagen Central Area showing how existing motorways, designed as part of the city plan for growth, terminate at the city boundary. Lights at the end of each road are under computer control, programmed to allow limited access by vehicles which the roads in the centre can handle.* Courtesy City of Copenhagen.

**Figure 76** *A typical radial motorway outside Copenhagen. Traffic in the morning rush hour can be held back for up to 15 minutes on these roads to allow a regulated flow onto the city's main roads. As in Singapore the system works well in the morning rush hour, but means that the roads are heavily congested in the evening peak period.* Courtesy Anders Nyvig A/S.

## CONTROLLED ENTRY

Copenhagen's five motorway access points on the west side of the city are equipped with programmed lights which 'meter' the traffic entering the internal road network, to the volume it can carry without becoming congested. The system in the morning peak requires cars to queue up for 10–15 minutes before entering. Nottingham tried a similar experiment in 1972 which held back cars at 'collars' and allowed buses

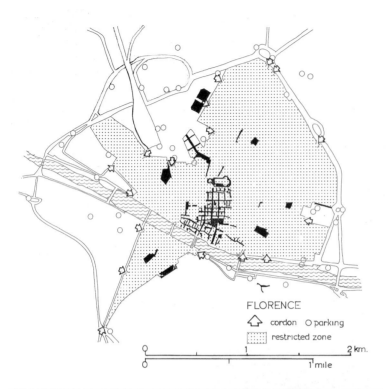

FLORENCE
△ cordon   O parking
▦ restricted zone

*Figure 77* Map of central Florence, showing the extent of the area banned to certain traffic. Residents' cars and those of visitors to hotels, taxis, buses and delivery vehicles are allowed in through any one of the 14 police-controlled checkpoints.

*Figure 78* View of a typical checkpoint where vehicles are diverted.

**Figure 79**  *Sign showing the type of vehicle allowed through.*

**Figure 80**  *Buses and taxis are allowed through.*

**Figure 81**  *Visitors to hotels are allowed through to drop off luggage.*

*The scheme, introduced in 1988, has reduced air pollution lby 20–30 per cent and has been already tried in Milan. The problem there has been the number of permits issued, so that the scheme has failed. Some towns, like Besançon in France, have carefully designated routes to hotels and limit long-term parking. Others, like Bologna and Siena, have politicians with the will to make the system work .*
Photos courtesy Pancini.

to pass through. This was withdrawn partially because of the lack of reservoir space for cars to wait.

Florence, a city of 440,000, introduced in 1988 traffic restrictions for its Central Area, which is around 4 km square (2 1/2 miles). Only cars belonging to residents and visitors to hotels, delivery vehicles, buses and taxis are permitted to drive through any one of the 15 control points which are manned by a total of around 30 police. All other cars are banned between 7.30 a.m. and 6.30 p.m. and from 9.20 p.m. to 1 a.m. Pollution levels have dropped by between 20 and 30 per cent since the introduction of the scheme.

# 7

# FREIGHT

Goods vehicles play an essential role in servicing the city, replenishing shops and offices with goods, or manufacturers and service industries with materials for assembly, which are then transported to other destinations, within or outside the city. Such activities generate a heavy demand on road space. For example, up to 20 per cent of vehicles on roads in London are occupied by goods vehicles. More critical, in recent years, has been the growth of heavy goods vehicles (HGVs) which comprise around 50 per cent of all freight traffic. Ideally those activities which generate large numbers of heavy vehicles should be relocated to fringe areas, preferably adjacent to railway sidings, canals and major roads where there is a choice of transport available, where they are less constrained by congestion, and where they cause less impact on the city environment.

Within the city, goods vehicles have considerable impact on the environment. A study (TRRL, 1973) on a typical shopping street in south London showed that goods vehicles represented 14 per cent of the vehicles on the street and were responsible for 60 per cent of noise over 85 dBA. However, their removal was estimated to reduce the noise level by only 1.5 dBA, because of the noise from buses. Studies on ways of reducing noise from heavy vehicles (TRRL, 1979) found that noise could be reduced by 10 dBA by suitable engine enclosure, combined with a change of tyre, at an increased vehicle cost of only 8 per cent. This principle could also be applied to buses, and has been carried out in Copenhagen successfully.

Not all heavy goods vehicles need to penetrate beyond the city boundaries. Paris, for example, has built freight complexes on the peripheral roads, where loads are broken down into smaller delivery sizes, destined for different parts of the city and carried by smaller trucks. Such complexes may be 20 hectares (50 acres) in size, have hotel, canteen and parking facilities and rented warehouse space for individual operators. Local trans-shipment depots are found in Holland serving towns of up to 250,000 people, where the Central Areas have been pedestrianised. Land is made available by the town, with a loan for private developers to build the town depot. Here 30 per cent of goods destined for the town are transferred onto a smaller distribution fleet of 2-ton lorries. The system works in both directions, with secure

**Figure 82** *Electric G-vans, under development in Southern California which have a top speed of 83 km/h (52 mph) and a range of 96 km (60 miles) on one battery charge. New legislation likely in the US will require that 10 per cent of the Federal Government's fleet of vehicles use alternative fuels, in up to 60 metropolitan areas. The new batteries being developed could lead, once this legislation is enforced, to electric power being more widely adopted.*
Courtesy Electric Vehicle Development Corporation.

short-term warehouse space being available for goods that are waiting to be transferred out of the town. Within cities, such a system organised by the local boroughs, but privately run, could help local distribution of non-perishable goods using electric vehicles.

Within pedestrian areas, authorities normally limit the times when service vehicles are allowed in, often up to 10 a.m. in Germany. Local distribution centres could help alleviate this, by allowing goods to be left for trans-shipment into the pedestrian area shops by small electric vehicle. The alternative to this is for side streets to be available and to be provided with service bays, such as is done in Cologne, where hand-trolleying of goods up to 30 metres (100 feet) is accepted by shopkeepers. The local distribution centre concept was studied (TRRL, 1976) with a view to serving Swindon town centre. It was discarded on the grounds of cost, without a proper evaluation of the side benefits which might be gained, such as the use of special electric vehicles for distribution (Plowden, 1980).

One alternative was tried for London in 1974 (Collins and Pharoah, 1974). It was called 'Operation Moondrop', and delivered goods between 6 p.m. and 10 p.m. Some firms reported a 20 per cent gain in travel speed, but found the overtime cost of staff to be excessive. Others running larger stores, who could have employed staff on regular night shifts on other activities, were more enthusiastic.

Some buildings – such as an exhibition centre, for example – within

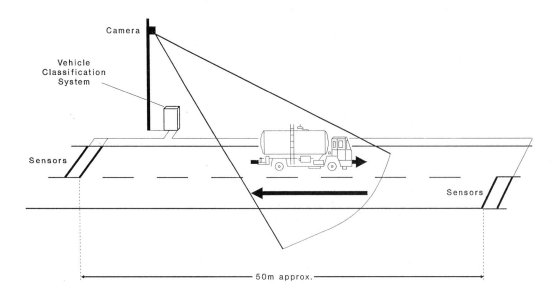

an existing city, may have only limited unloading space. Where moving to a new site is not an option, means have to be found to overcome the servicing problem. At Brighton, where the annual Traffex Exhibition is held, there is space at the conference centre, on the seafront, for only eight to ten vehicles to unload at the rear. Here the municipality rents a former abattoir as a vehicle-holding area, supervised by a traffic controller, in radio contact with the unloading area, and up to 200 vehicles are served in a day at a cost of £10 per vehicle, paid to the municipality.

The increasing use of 38-ton freight vehicles requires that designated lorry routes are provided within the city. In residential areas a ban on access by them is frequently made, and essential, unless certain land uses can show grounds for allowing access. Dutch towns deliberately restrain entry by HGVs, by placing posts 30 cm (12 inches) closer together than the legal limit. Night-time bans in cities on lorries are also normal, with Stockholm banning entry from 10 p.m. to 6 a.m. London has a ban on all vehicles over 16.5 tons on metropolitan roads from 9 p.m. to 7 a.m. on weekdays, except for those carrying highly perishable goods.

Lorry routes were planned in 1974 for London, in a study by the

*Figure 83* *A device under trial in the UK for the Transport and Road Research Laboratory aimed at ensuring roads are not used by overweight freight vehicles. Sensors built into the road bed are connected to a roadside computer which classifies the type of vehicle, records its length, and determines the maximum load it should be carrying. If overweight, a camera photographs the number plate and records the time of day it passed.*
Courtesy Castle Rock Consultants, Nottingham.

*Figure 84a* A road-narrowing scheme in a residential area of London designed to limit the size of vehicles entering. Dutch towns frequently restrain heavy vehicles from entering by placing posts on each side of the road 300 mm (12 inches) closer than the legal limit.

*Figure 84b (right)* View of double handling for goods which occurs in Venice, Italy. Goods pass from truck to barge at the periphery, then onto a variety of hand trolleys designed to suit the goods handled. While adding to the cost of goods, and the cost of living, this still retains a civilised environment and one not dominated by deliveries.

*Figure 84c (left)* Electric vehicles used for deliveries in Zermatt, Switzerland. A resort town which has banned cars from entering and uses electric vehicles in its centre.

A central delivery depot could serve a sector of a city centre which has been pedestrianised, eliminating the need for truck deliveries to individual shops or offices. An electric vehicle fleet could be used as in Zermatt, and so eliminate pollution from diesel fumes. Such depots are being used successfully in two Dutch towns and are privately run.

GLC (Collins and Pharoah, 1974), proposing that around 680 kms (425 miles) of road would be designated for their use. However, objections made by residents, and others, along 30 per cent of these roads resulted in the scheme being dropped. Had grants been made available for double glazing, combined with financial compensation to owners of property, the scheme might have been more easily accepted. Today with strong opposition to new road building the proposal urgently needs reviewing.

Research is being carried out in the UK to find ways of checking and enforcing loading, while the vehicle is moving to avoid overweight vehicles using roads. Sensors are built into the road bed, which pass information to a roadside computer, trigger a camera and record the vehicle number plate and the time at which it passed. Freight vehicles are being better designed, to enable them to be loaded more easily, with air-cushion floors, to facilitate the movement of pallets. Others now run articulated outside the city, but can be split into two trailers, for distribution within, powered by two separate vehicles.

Finally, there is the important factor of reducing road congestion, to allow freight to move more easily. Some bus lanes could be usefully shared, provided there was spare capacity. Road-pricing freight vehicles in central areas would encourage the consolidation of goods outside the cordon area and the use of local distribution centres, served by electric vehicles, which would be exempt from road-pricing.

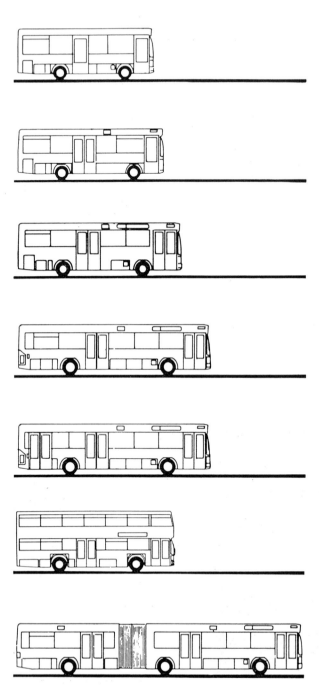

**Figure 85** *Diagram showing the range of buses manufactured by Neoplan, West Germany, designed with low floor levels for easy boarding.*
Courtesy Neoplan.

# 8

# BUSES

All cities use buses, either as their principal means of public transport, or with other systems, such as light rail or rapid transit. In recent years buses have suffered from a poor image. They have been submerged in traffic congestion, causing unreliable services to be run, with a consequent loss of passengers. In recent years, many cities, notably Paris and Copenhagen, have overcome this problem by providing bus lanes and bus priorities at street junctions, allowing buses to run unimpeded and provide reliable services. Bus design, too, has played an important part in upgrading the image of buses.

## THE VEHICLE RANGE

A wide range of vehicle size is available, to meet demand, and authorities are more prepared to experiment with different bus designs, to provide more efficient operation. For example, tickets are often pre-purchased and the bus designed with more doors and low floors to reduce boarding time at stops.

*Figure 86* The Neoplan articulated bus showing the ease in boarding through wide doors for a passenger from the kerb edge.
Articulated buses are now being widely used on busy corridors, with 50 seats and room for 106 standing, a lower seating capacity than a double decker, but reducing the time spent boarding and leaving at stops.
Courtesy Neoplan.

**Figures 87, 88** *Denver, Colorado uses specially-built low-loading buses by Vetter, for distributing passengers along its 1.6 km (1 mile) long pedestrian mall. A total of 19 mall buses are used, 7 diesel and 6 electric, running at 70-second intervals in each direction from the bus terminals at each end. Ridership is around 40,000 per day and the service is free.*
Courtesy Smithson.

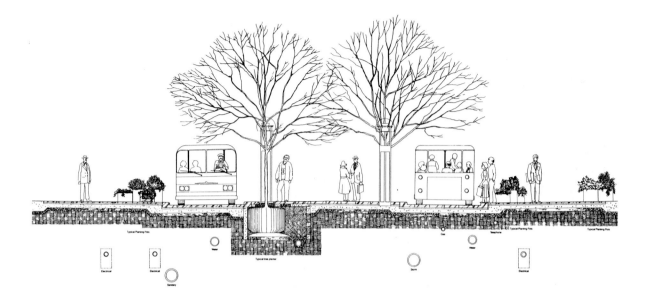

## Minibuses

In the UK, largely because of deregulation, discussed below, there has been an increased use of minibuses by private operators, with around 5000 operating, mostly serving low-density areas. They seat from 15 to 25 people, and can frequently be hailed to stop at any point. They are of low cost, between £15,000 and £20,000 each, with maintenance costs around a sixth of those for a conventional bus, and need to carry an estimated 32 passengers per bus hour, 380 per day, to break even (Turner and White, 1987). Minibuses are used in London on a dial-a-ride basis to serve disabled people and are equipped with special low-boarding facilities. The low capacity and small size of the minibus make it more manoeuvrable on narrow roads and an increased frequency, compared with a conventional bus, has been found to attract passengers (White, 1986). There are many attractive minibuses now in production and it is possible to have them built to serve a wide range of needs. For example, 13 specially-designed minibuses are used, six electric and seven diesel powered, in the shopping mall at Denver, Colorado, with low-boarding facilities and six doors, and run at 70-second intervals as a free shuttle service carrying over 40,000 shoppers a day from the bus stations at each end of the 1.6 km (1 mile) long mall.

*Figure 89* Design drawing of Denver mall showing specially-designed street lighting, tree-planting, central reservation for pedestrians over part of the mall, pavements surfaced in two colours of granite and the two bus-only lanes.
Courtesy I.M. Pei Architects and Planners.

### Midibuses

London Transport launched high-frequency midibuses in 1989, carrying 28 seated and 15 standing passengers. These are radio-controlled and on some routes hail-and-ride services are used.

### Standard buses

These are being built to a higher specification with wide doors and facilities for access by disabled people and carry from 40 to 60 passengers. Buses have been developed by Scania and Volvo, for Copenhagen, which use a built-in flywheel, releasing the energy from breaking for subsequent acceleration, and result in fuel economies of 28 per cent. The low noise level on all buses in Copenhagen is particularly interesting and the result of special studies by the manufacturers.

### Trolleybuses

There is a revival of interest in trolleybuses, principally in Europe and South America. Nancy, in France, has recently completed a new installation, and in the UK Bradford is proposing to install a 41 km (25 1/2 mile) system, over a hilly route, which is estimated to reduce exhaust emissions by 71.7 tonnes a year. Many new trolleybuses are dual-mode, equipped with diesel motors for use at special junctions or maintenance depots. They have operating costs around 75 per cent of diesel buses and a life from 25 to 35 years compared with 15 years for a diesel bus. In Nancy, for example, their noise levels are between 10 and 30 dBA quieter than diesel buses, with speeds around 14 per cent higher.

### Guided buses

Two recent installations have been completed in Essen, and in Adelaide, South Australia, with a 19 km (12 mile) track which uses guided buses. The buses are standard city service articulated vehicles, developed by Mercedes-Benz, and are provided with three pairs of solid rubber-tyred guide rollers on each side. The bus, which runs along an ordinary road enters the track, which has the ends splayed, at 40 km/h (25 mph). The driver releases the steering wheel on entering, and can drive the bus safely at speeds of up to 100 km/h (62 mph). An estimated capacity of 18,000 passengers per hour could be achieved with no intermediate stations. In Adelaide over 11 bus routes converge from different suburban routes on the guideway, which carries more than 15,000 passengers a day, reducing total journey times from 33 to

***Figure 90*** *Diagrams showing how an O-Bahn, a guided bus system, could be upgraded in stages.*

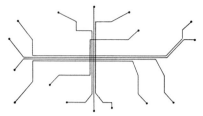

*Today.*

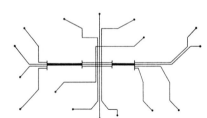

*Stage 1: the guidance track in use over two parts of the track.*

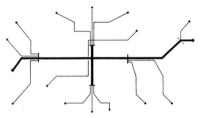

*Stage 2: the introduction of a total system using a duo-bus, possibly running in tunnel below the Central Area under electric power.*
Courtesy Daimler-Benz

*Figure 91* A typical O-Bahn in Essen leaving a tunnel shared with trams in the centre and running on its guidance track. In the suburbs the bus will leave its guidance track and circulate in the residential areas under diesel power. Courtesy Daimler-Benz.

*Figure 92 (left)* Guided bus in Essen showing how the driver releases the steering wheel on entering the track at speed, taking it over as he leaves the track.

*Figure 93 (right)* A typical guidance wheel on an Essen bus. Each articulated bus has three wheels on each side directly connected to the power steering.

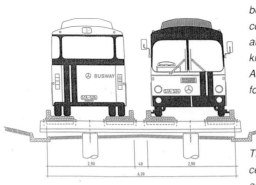

*Figure 94* Comparison in cross-section between  guided bus (O-Bahn, top) and conventional busways (typical, centre and preferred, bottom). Costs for the 19-km (12-mile) track in Adelaide, South Australia, were only slightly above those for a conventional busway.

The O-Bahn system's advantage in city centres is that a two-way system is around 3 metres (10 feet) narrower than a conventional busway, and Hamburg is now considering introducing the system on a radial and busily used corridor for this reason.

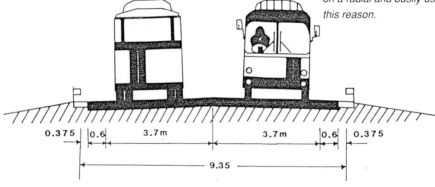

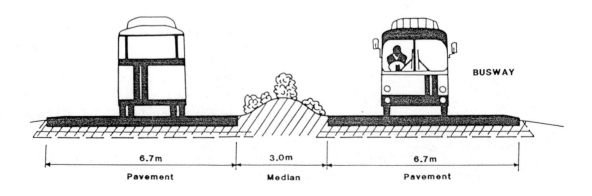

Bus routes entering at Paradise
Bus routes entering at Tea Tree Plaza
Busway stop
City centre access route
Other inter-connecting bus routes

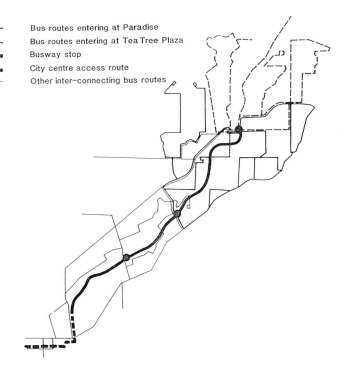

*Figure 95* Adelaide, South Australia. Plan of guidance track 19 km (12 miles) long used by guided buses with entry points. Travel times have been reduced from 33 to 23 minutes since its completion and park-and-ride patrons have steadily increased.

*Figure 96* A typical section of Adelaide busway running at grade, with a piled foundation due to sub-surface conditions. Buses can cruise at 100 km/h (62 mph) and enter the track at around 40 km/h (25 mph). Standard and articulated buses are used which circulate in the residential areas before entering the busway and the system carries around 12,000 passengers on a weekday.

*Figure 97* An elevated section of a busway has been integrated into River Torrens Linear Park, an important conservation area, providing flood relief measures and cycle and pedestrian paths integrated into the landscape.

Courtesy North-east Busway Project Team, Adelaide.

3 minutes. Estimated capital costs of the guided busway system are 30 per cent lower than light rail, with added flexibility, and only 10 per cent more than the cost of a conventional bus.

## Articulated buses

These are manufactured by several companies, worldwide, with a range of seating and standing space available to suit requirements. They have certain advantages over double deckers, although they have fewer seats, and as a result need less time for leaving and boarding at stops. In a study undertaken for Sheffield in the UK, a bus carrying 135 people, using all four doors, could exit all passengers in 23 seconds.

## BUS PRIORITY

Measures are essential to ensure that buses receive priority over other traffic, if they are to be attractive to passengers. Traffic management, generally aimed at maximising road space, must ensure that buses are properly considered. One-way streets, for example, should have counter-flow bus lanes, so that bus routes are not split, but remain comprehensible for passengers. At light-controlled intersections, busy bus lanes should continue up to the lights with no setback, as is often done; the lights can then be changed by a transponder on the bus, an electronic device which provides a beam to a kerbside beacon and so operates the lights in favour of the bus, giving it a right of way over other traffic.

*Figure 98* Bus lanes in Hamburg formerly a tram right-of-way. The shortage of space requires that the bus stops are staggered or made very narrow but, as shown (above the railway bridge), can share pedestrian crossings. Buses are fitted with 'transponders', devices which turn the traffic lights in their favour as they approach a junction.
Courtesy Hamburg HUV.

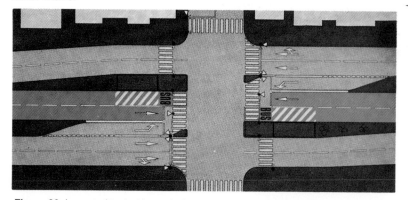

*Figure 99* Layout of typical bus priority road in Paris, showing integration of pedestrian crossing. Turning traffic is held and the bus given priority to pass through.
Courtesy RATP Paris.

**Figure 100(a)** *Key route' busways in Nagoya, Japan, started in 1985 with two 10 km (6.2 miles) long routes. The busway shown serves morning and evening peak period at 1–2 minute intervals (45 buses per hour) with buses running at average speeds of 25 km/h (15 mph). Traffic signals are controlled to suit bus operation.*

**Figure 100(b)** *A typical bus stop, located in centre of road, each with information boards connected to central control showing passengers where their bus is and when it will arrive.* Courtesy City of Nagoya.

## BUSWAYS

Paris is continually extending its busways with 304 km (190 miles) of busways out of 518 km (324 miles) of route in inner Paris, partly because of the scale of its boulevards. In Copenhagen, all main roads in the centre have exclusive busways, beside cycle tracks, and these are often separated from other traffic by 300-mm (12-inch) wide, shaped kerbs. No street parking or unloading is permitted on any of these roads. In some city centres, such as Philadelphia and Portland, Oregon, exclusive two-way bus-only roads have been built, which are well-landscaped and provide an overall environmental improvement.

## INFORMATION SYSTEMS

Buses can now be equipped with systems which enable their position to be determined from a central control point. In the event of breakdown, or hold-up in traffic, more buses can be put on to a route. Short-wave cab radios are satisfactory for up to 100 buses on one channel, but larger fleets use more advanced systems (White, 1986). London, like many cities, uses BUSCO, where loops are set in the road and bus-mounted sensors pick up signals from below, automatically decoded and transmitted to the control centre. Future systems may rely on beacons which allow bus routes to be more easily changed. Once a central controller has information on the location of all the buses, information can be relayed electronically to passengers at the bus stop, telling them the time of arrival of the next bus. In Hanover, feeder buses at the light-rail terminal stations are equipped with automatic vehicle monitoring systems, identical to those on the light-rail vehicle. Their time of arrival can, as a result, coincide and cross-platform interchange be made by passengers with no waiting.

## DEREGULATION

This is a British phenomenon, introduced as part of government policy in 1980, and resulted in the privatisation of the bus industry, outside London. It has meant that, in many towns and cities, a free for all by different operators has occurred, not unlike the American jitneys of 1925, and has generally resulted in a loss of passengers. However, not all the results have been bad. Minibuses have been used by operators to reduce running and capital costs, and offer, on some routes, more frequent services. The problem lies in the lack of co-ordination between

**Figure 101(a)** *Passenger information display board at Nice using Serel's Busco system informing passengers where the next bus is located on route.*

**Figure 101(b)** *Buses are equipped with sensors which pick up signals from loops set in the road. These are converted to signals and transmitted automatically to the control centre, where the bus's progress is monitored. Display screens show if the bus is running on time. The display boards at bus stops are connected by telephone line to the control centre and the information given reduces the 'apparent' waiting time of passengers.*
Courtesy Serel France.

**Figure 102(a)** *A typical bus control centre in Holland using the Vecom automatic vehicle monitoring system which identifies buses on each route, recording if they are running on time, or if they are fully loaded. Buses can have sensoring devices at doors and exits which count passenger flows and monitor whether more buses should be put onto a certain route.*
Courtesy Philips Telecommunications and Information Systems.

services, and the risk that services will not run in the future along routes which are less profitable. The approach, now used in London and some German cities, to put some routes out to tender in certain areas, is preferable and so allows some control by the central authority, as well as reducing the operating costs.

## THE FUTURE

Planning for better bus operation has, in recent years, encouraged passengers in all European countries, except the UK, back on to buses, particularly where busways are provided, to allow bus companies to run a reliable service. However, diesel buses pollute and their fumes are carcinogenic – virtually pure carbon – which can be inhaled and deposited in the lungs. (A recent Harvard University study shows that people regularly exposed to diesel exhaust may be 42 per cent more likely to develop cancer.) Experiments with electric buses have failed, because a satisfactory battery is still unavailable, and not

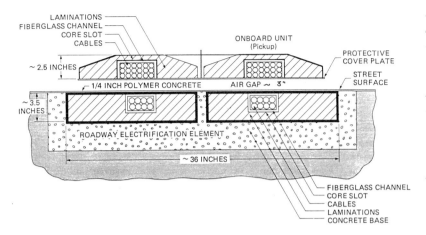

LAMINATIONS
FIBERGLASS CHANNEL
CORE SLOT
CABLES
ONBOARD UNIT
(Pickup)
PROTECTIVE
COVER PLATE
~ 2.5 INCHES
STREET
SURFACE
1/4 INCH POLYMER CONCRETE
AIR GAP ~ 3"
~ 3.5
INCHES
ROADWAY ELECTRIFICATION ELEMENT
~ 36 INCHES
FIBERGLASS CHANNEL
CORE SLOT
CABLES
LAMINATIONS
CONCRETE BASE

*Figures 102b, 102c* Prototype electric bus under trial at Richmond Field Station, University of California, part of the Programme on Advanced Technology for the Highway (PATH). A continuous element, embedded in the street surface, provides electrical energy to the bus by means of an electromagnetic induction principle called 'inductive coupling', which takes place, as the drawing shows, across an air gap of 75 mm (3 inches). There is no hazard for pedestrians walking across the cable. Once road beds in a city, possibly starting in the central area, are electrified in this way, other electric vehicles equipped with an onboard pick-up unit could use it and so eliminate pollution. Long-term implications are that small, driverless electric buses such as these could run fully automated on roads equipped with cabling and deliver or collect people door to door, using similarly equipped transitways for longer distance travel.
Courtesy Howard Ross.

*Feeder buses represent an essential part of any fixed-track system and need to make the interchange for passengers as easy as possible, if they are to be attracted from using cars to public transport.*

*With higher densities and close station spacing of up to 640 metres (700 yards), stations can be within walking distance of homes of workplaces. Feeder buses must, however, run frequently, on time and be closely co-ordinated with train or tram arrival times, reducing waiting to the minimum.*

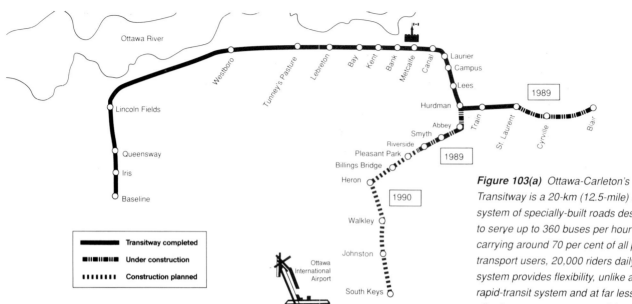

*Figure 103(a)* Ottawa-Carleton's Transitway is a 20-km (12.5-mile) long system of specially-built roads designed to serve up to 360 buses per hour and carrying around 70 per cent of all public transport users, 20,000 riders daily. The system provides flexibility, unlike a rapid-transit system and at far less cost, allowing passengers to travel from their local bus stop to the city centre without interchanging. Shopping centres, businesses and residential developments are being planned around stations outside the central area. Here a transit mall is planned and as the city grows, buses may be put in tunnel below the centre.

Legend:
- ▬▬▬ Transitway completed
- ▰▮▰▮▰ Under construction
- ▪▪▪▪▪ Construction planned

*Figure 103(b)* East Transitway running in cutting.

*Figure 103(c)* Lincoln Fields station with bus entering the Transitway. Courtesy Ottawa-Carleton Transit Commission Photos Penson.

sufficiently in demand. Interesting work is being done in California, where the feasibility and economies of collecting current from the road bed are being tried, and which, if successful, could mean that all urban vehicles could be powered from this source. Overhead wires and trolleybuses are the alternative. All the other requirements necessary for good bus operations are available today: the provision of comfortable heated shelters, information systems for passengers and the track for buses.

# 9 INTERCHANGES

The travelling public dislikes interchanging and any ideal transport network avoids the need for interchange. In practice, this is more likely in medium-sized cities – perhaps up to 500,000, where buses are the principal means of public transport. In large cities where several different systems are used, often 50 per cent of trips require interchange (Bell, 1976).

The principal requirements for planning an interchange can be summarised as follows:

1 Simplicity is the keynote of success. A clear plan, easily comprehended where only simple, clear signing is necessary.
2 Through-ticketing is ideal, allowing passengers to change systems and avoid wasting time at machines or ticket offices.
3 Comfortable conditions are necessary, weather-protected and free from overcrowding. In a new interchange, dimensions of platforms, stair and waiting areas should be capable of handling peak flows, and of being enlarged as traffic increases. In underground construction this is vital, as to do this later is very expensive.
4 Walking distances should be kept to the minimum. Some authorities place a value of walking time at twice to three times 'in vehicle' time (Wagon and Collins, 1973). Where distances are over 200 metres (670 feet) in underground passages, pedestrian conveyors should be used. In Paris, the Métro has six conveyors all over 10 metres (33 feet) long to cut walking time by 50 per cent (Richards, 1976).
5 Escalators should be provided where there are changes of level above 4 metres (13 feet), at least for the upward climb, as well as stairs which need to be at least half as wide again as the passages approaching them (Turner, 1959). In underground construction this is frequently overlooked, to simplify construction, and cut costs.
6 Waiting areas should be well lit, with seats, and in busy stations provided with useful shops, sited behind ticket barriers – a boon to passengers, and only requiring limited servicing arrangements.
7 Electronic real-time information boards are required on platforms and waiting areas to inform passengers accurately how long they have to wait. In Newcastle in a survey at an interchange, 75 per

cent of passengers said they would use the bus again because of the information system, and said that knowing when buses were arriving helped to pass waiting time (Sheldon, 1985).

8   Frequency and reliability of service are essential, to avoid waiting at an interchange. This means a close co-ordination between different systems (see Bus – Rail below).

All the interchanges discussed below have similar characteristics and all require that people walk. In Europe, a high proportion of trips to bus stops or rail stations is made on foot because of close spacing of stops or stations and the density of development, and in London, of all people travelling daily on the Underground, 76 per cent walk to stations.

## BUS–RAIL

Feeder buses collect and deliver passengers from stops beyond walking distance from stations. In London, and in other cities, minibuses or midibuses are being tried, which run at greater frequency than conventional buses, say five minutes instead of ten, and are preferred by passengers. In Hanover, at the light-rail terminal stations, buses are equipped with the same computerised automatic vehicle monitoring systems as the trams, and both are co-ordinated, via a central control room, to arrive at the same time for cross-platform interchange. (Deregulation of buses makes this kind of technology and co-ordination unlikely.)

Elevated rapid-transit, as in Washington DC suburban stations, has island platforms, with stairs and lift, to a covered area below, where feeder buses can unload adjacent to station entrances. In Paris, at one terminal station – Gallieni – situated at a junction on the peripheral motorway, covered unloading is provided for 22 buses at a time, with access direct to Métro platform level.

## BUS–BUS

Normally this requires no change of level, but adequate space. Bus-only roads, as used on one route in Hamburg, with low volumes, and around 3-minute frequency, use long island platforms in the centre of the main road. Local buses drop passengers, who walk along to pick-up express buses at the same stop. With high volumes of buses, such as in Porto Allegre, Brazil, where flows exceed 350 buses per hour,

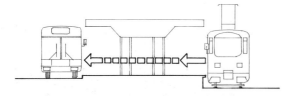

**Figure 104**  Typical cross-platform interchange between bus and light rail used at terminal stations on the H-Bahn in Hanover.

**Figure 105**  A station platform.

Feeder buses represent an essential part of any fixed-track system and need to make the interchange for passengers as easy as possible, if they are to be attracted from using cars to public transport. With higher densities and close station spacing of up to 640 metres (700 yards), stations can be within walking distance of homes of workplaces. Feeder buses must however run frequently, be on time and be closely co-ordinated with train or tram arrival times, reducing waiting to the minimum.

**Figure 106**  Driver's on-board LED (liquid display) boards on Hanover's USTRA light-rail cars which, via the central control room, inform the driver if he is running on time. Buses are fitted with identical boards to co-ordinate arrival times for passengers interchanging.

special interchange terminals are provided which are 'controlled areas' to allow feeder bus passengers to make cross-platform interchange with express buses and use the same ticket. In Edmonton, Alberta, 17 transit centres are used in the suburbs, some of which are planned as part of local shopping centres. Each is served by five to ten bus routes, which are co-ordinated to arrive within three to five minutes of buses leaving on other routes, using a system called pulse scheduling. Interchange is at ground level, with any necessary waiting done within the weather-controlled shopping centre, where real-time information boards inform passengers when a bus is about to leave (Cervero, 1986).

*Figure 107* *Rhode Island Avenue interchange station, Washington DC which has a staggered kerb line and wide pavements to allow for queuing, only partly under cover. The central island platform is served by lift for disabled people. Free two-hour transfer passes from bus to rail are issued to passengers.*
Photo WMTA.

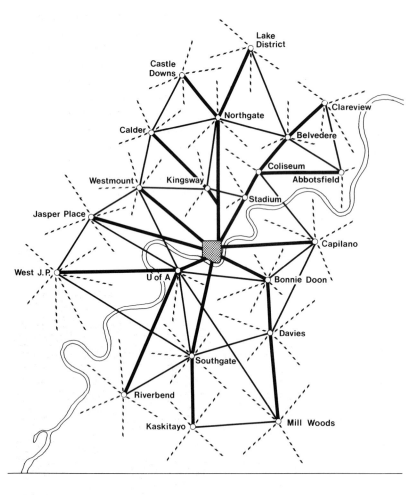

*Figure 108* Plan of Edmonton, Alberta, showing the location of transit centres served by buses. The system provides cross-city movement to transit centres situated at strategic points, such as a shopping centre, University or light-rail stop. Only 22.5 per cent of Edmonton's work force is located in the central area and the system is designed to serve those trips normally made by car.

| | |
|---|---|
| ▬▬ Mainline Corridors | - - - Feeder Routes |
| ▬ Crosstown Routes | ○ Transit Centres |

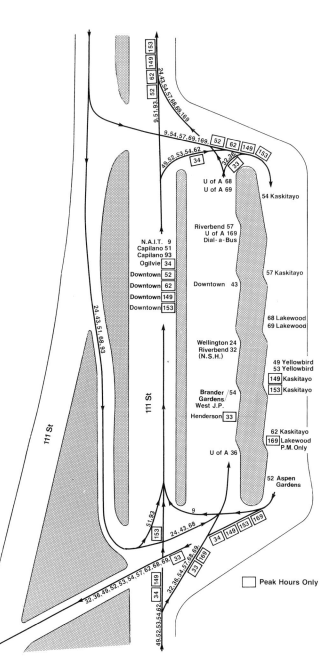

N.A.I.T. 9
Capilano 51
Capilano 93
Ogilvie 34
Downtown 52
Downtown 62
Downtown 149
Downtown 153

U of A 68
U of A 69

54 Kaskitayo

Riverbend 57
U of A 169
Dial-a-Bus

57 Kaskitayo

Downtown 43

68 Lakewood
69 Lakewood

Wellington 24
Riverbend 32
(N.S.H.)

49 Yellowbird
53 Yellowbird
149 Kaskitayo
153 Kaskitayo

Brander /54
Gardens
West J.P.

Henderson 33

62 Kaskitayo
169 Lakewood
P.M. Only

U of A 36

52 Aspen
Gardens

Peak Hours Only

111 St

**Figures 109, 110** *Plan and view of typical bus transfer point in Edmonton allows for cross-platform interchange on many of the routes. Buses arrive at 10–15 minute frequencies and are scheduled to reduce waiting time to the minimum. The stations are provided with covered, heated waiting areas, some of which are part of the shopping mall and real-time information boards inform passengers of arrivals.*
Courtesy Edmonton Transit

## RAIL-RAIL

In London, around 46 per cent of Underground passengers make one interchange and 7 per cent make two, to reach their destination. In planning additional new lines these are, where structurally feasible, often planned to allow for cross-platform interchange to take place between two lines. This method is ideal, but can be problematic when large numbers are interchanging. For example, Hong Kong, in planning its new metro, has three interchange stations where cross-platform interchange takes place on each line, through changing the level of the tracks. However, because of the constraints from the buildings above, dimensions have proved to give insufficient reservoir space on the platforms should an incoming train be delayed – understandable in a stations where 250,000 passengers interchange in one day!

In existing stations where two kinds of lines cross, for example, long-distance commuting and local metro, behind-barrier interchange is important for ticket holders. The newly completed Métro Régional in Paris has eliminated the need for interchange at mainline stations on some suburban lines, by constructing new tunnels across the centre to carry these lines, interchanging at only a few key stations with the local metro. London's Crossrail, planned to open in eight years, will provide a similar service running east–west and relieve the presently overloaded Central Line.

## PARK-AND-RIDE

### Cycles

The most modest and economic form of park-and-ride, in terms of economy and convenience, is cycling. In Copenhagen, 15 per cent of suburban rail passengers use cycles between home and station, in a city which has a policy of not providing car parks at stations. In Holland, around 90,000 cycles are parked under cover at 1100 of the larger stations, managed and supervised by a separate company for a daily fee. Japan has an annual growth rate of cycle traffic of around 20 per cent with more than 6000 cycles parked at some stations, both underground and in multi-storeyed parks, with around a 50 cent daily fee charged (Grabe and Utech, 1984).

Where extensive access by cycles occurs, special provision has to be made with cycleways and junction improvements, to provide a safe right of way (see Cycling).

## Cars

Many city authorities see park-and-ride as a way of reducing the pressure for road-building and car parking within a central area. In small cities such as Oxford, UK (population 110,000), park-and-ride at four peripheral points, 2–3 km (1–2 miles) from the centre, with parking for a total of 2300 cars, has proved popular with commuters and shoppers (Bixby, 1986). This has reduced the need for increasing the present 2400 spaces in the centre, and successfully kept over 1 million cars a year out. A bus fleet of nine vehicles running at 10–15 minute intervals is used with a return fare of 50p, covering the parking charge.

Hamburg, since 1973, has actively pursued a park-and-ride policy over distances of 5 km (3 miles) from the central area (where parking for 30,000 cars has now been frozen). Two new multi-storey parks are complete south of the city, each for 500 cars with direct access by lift to platform level, paid for by a combination of Federal and City grants. In contrast to this, Toronto intends to remove 35 per cent of its total park-and-ride, now around 4000 spaces, to new 'gateway' sites further out,

**Figure 111** *Multi-storey park-and-ride car park for over 1000 cars at Torcy, Paris, served by the RER (Métro Express) running across the city centre. It is part of the infrastructure being built to provide 100,000 car spaces at points on the periphery. By being multi-storeyed, walking distances to trains are reduced, although in this case require drivers to cross the access road.* Courtesy RATP.

adjoining major roads and peripheral metro or express bus stations. By doing this, the parking areas can be redeveloped commercially because of the rise in land values around stations (Toronto Transit Commission, 1988). Vancouver, with its recently completed 'Skytrain' has not provided 'park-and-ride' at its stations, because of high land costs, but will do so later when its extension is completed, on inexpensive land at the edge of the city.

In London, with 146,000 park-and-ride spaces, relatively few spaces are provided within the North and South Circular roads as a matter of policy, to avoid 'railheading' – where commuters drive in and park as close as they can to the centre to reduce their rail fares. Many residential areas have licensed residents-only parking for the same reason – effective in keeping out commuters. However, with the completion of the M25 outer circular road, already carrying traffic flows predicted for AD 2000, more park-and-ride is needed, outside this, linked direct to improved rail lines. If 5000 park-and-ride spaces were built, plus a road-pricing policy implemented in the central area, this is estimated to reduce cars commuting into it by 3 per cent (LPAC, 1989), still a disappointingly low figure, partly because of the amount of free private parking in the centre.

Park-and-ride uses valuable land and requires to be carefully integrated into the landscape to be acceptable. Access road have to be adequately scaled, and multi-storey parks, although costing around £5500 per car space, have the advantage of being compact and avoid long walks from the car to train – or express bus stops. However, there seems no reason why park-and-ride should be entirely paid for by the city, and it could at least partly be privately financed from a central fund into which all developers building new schemes within a city could contribute. London, notoriously backward in this respect, could, with advantage, adopt such a policy. However, it will not do so until an overall transportation plan is made. Munich has successfully adopted a strategy where underground parking costs around £15,000 per space, and developers who do not want to pay this pay an exemption fee of around £3000 per car space into the municipal parking fund, put towards parking outside the inner ring road, now amounting to some £10 million (OECD, 1988).

**Kiss-and-ride**

Spouses are given a lift from home to station or bus stop, and drop-down areas are provided in new stations, close to entrances. Toronto, at Finch station, has provided a circular ring road around a special drop-down point, which can handle 100 cars where passengers can wait in an enclosed area.

Park-and-ride is worth pursuing if by its introduction parking levels in the inner city can either be 'frozen' or, better still, reduced and so bring a positive benefit to the environment. This could mean a reduction, or elimination in some areas, of on-street parking, except for car parks for disabled people, pavement widening and tree-planting. Strict measures against illegal parking have also to be applied and public car parks ideally turned over to short-term use. Park-and-ride is of particular value to car-borne passengers, commuters and shoppers living outside the city, and requires high-speed links into the city by rail, or express bus, to succeed in reducing the pressure for increased access by private car into the city centre.

# 10
# RAIL

The systems discussed in this chapter have a common characteristic, that of running on tracks. Each system can run elevated, on segregated track (or semi-segregated track for light rail) at ground level or underground, unimpeded by vehicular traffic, at high-average operating speeds of up to 35 km/h (22 mph). Their environmental impact in terms of noise level and visual intrusion applies in particular to the elevated systems. All the systems, being electric, are non-polluting. They carry from 15,000 to 60,000 passengers per hour and are designed to serve, if considered from a solely economic point of view, high density corridors of movement, to justify the high cost of their construction. In practice there may be other reasons, usually political, which decide on their construction.

Three types of rail systems are discussed:

1  Rapid transit or metro. A high-speed, often automated, high-capacity system, with on-board attendant, carrying 40,000–60,000 passengers per hour, at average speeds of 30 km/h (18.5 mph). Stations are around 1–2 km (1 mile) apart, or 500–600 metres (1/3 mile) in Central Areas.
2  Light rail transit. An advanced driver-operated tram, running on its own right of way, with stops around 500-1000 metres (1/2 mile), carrying up to 15,000 passengers per hour at an average speed of 20 km/h (121/2 mph) .
3  Advanced light transit. A range of new systems which are fully automated, without drivers, running at average speeds of up to 22 mph (35 km/h). Stations are at 1/2-mile (500–1000-metre) intervals and the capacity is around 20,000 passengers per hour in each direction.

## RAPID TRANSIT

This has largely been responsible for the pattern of growth in densely built cities such as London, where, following rail lines, the underground provided close station spacing at 1.6–3 km (1–2 mile) intervals in the suburbs, effectively filling in the land between railway stations with residential development. Rapid transit such as the system which opened in Hong Kong in 1979 is designed to serve dense corridors of movement carrying over 500 million people a year, but this example is unique. The American experience, however, is a lesson which can be learned, with advantage, by many cities in the developing world now considering building rapid-transit systems.

Generally, rapid transit provides too great a capacity for most travel corridors, except at peak hours. For example, San Francisco's BART system carries only 230,000 people on an average weekday on its 115-km (75-mile) long system (53 million passengers a year) and serves an estimated 5 per cent of peak hour trips in the region (Hall, 1980). It runs, however, through hilly terrain and across water, so that were it not for high car ownership it could have worked. Instead, the freeway system, had it been designed with segregated bus lanes, could have provided a better solution. Conventional rapid transit is now recognised as an expensive way of providing public transport, and many cities in recent years have held back, and are considering less costly alternatives, using buses, or light rail, which can provide more extensive networks, at less cost.

The exceptions are cities such as Paris and London, where rapid transit already exists, is overloaded, and where more lines are required to relieve congestion on existing ones.

## The technology

Rapid-transit systems use from two to ten cars coupled together to form trains, depending on the demand. Each carries up to 50 seated and 50 standing passengers per car, running at top speeds of 80-100 km/h (50-60 mph) which, with stops at 1000 metre (5/8 mile) intervals, gives an average operating speed of 30 km/h (18 mph). Trains are now frequently fully automated, with an attendant on board, for emergencies, or for controlling doors at stations. Tunnelling is normally done below central areas, where station spacing is ideally reduced to 500-metre (500–600-yard) intervals. The tunnel construction, and its depth, depend on soil conditions (Vuchic, 1981). Shallow tunnels using advanced 'cut and cover' methods allow them to be quickly covered over, and are built often following the main roads above. In planning terms this allows station platforms to be more easily reached by passengers, and entrances can be better located at street level. Deep bored tunnels, as used in London, can be freed from the road pattern above, but have to avoid the piled foundations of tall buildings. They require long escalators, meaning a loss of passenger time. Outside the central area, grade level stations and tracks are rarely built, because of

the severance caused, and elevated tracks on special structures, or embankments, are normal, although special provision has to be made to reduce noise. Generally, tunnelling costs up to eight times, and elevated track about three times more than the cost of an 'at grade' system.

## Standards

Many newly-built transit systems, as in Washington DC, are models of good design, and have set new space standards. For example, subway pedestrian passages in New York and London, were designed at a standard of 82 people per metre per minute (25–27 people per foot per minute) while for the Washington metro they are designed at a standard of 45 people per metre per minute (13.6 people per foot per

*Figure 112* View of Châtelet station at Les Halles, the largest underground station in Paris, with new lines for the Métro Express and the Métro Régional. The photo gives some idea of the magnitude of inserting such a system into an existing historic city and cause the minimum of interruption to the street. Courtesy RATP.

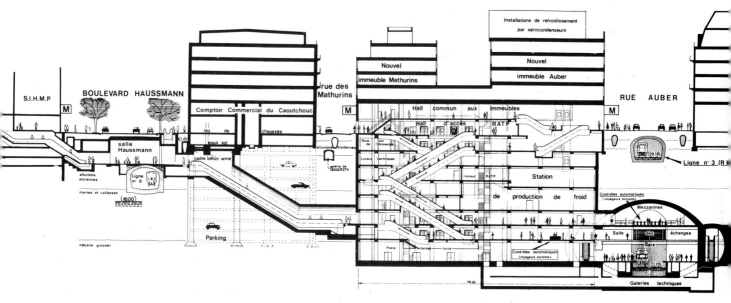

**Figure 114** *Cross-section through Auber station, Paris, showing the two original metro lines below boulevard Haussmann and rue Auber (Lines 3 and 9), and the new RER Métro Express running deep below rue Auber served by two separate concourses for incoming and outgoing passengers. The new building constructed provides apartments on four floors above, a department store below and an escalator linking Line 9 which turns into a conveyor at the bottom.*
Courtesy RATP.

**Figure 113** *Tokyo subway at Shinjuku, one of the largest interchanges where 1 million passengers change trains daily in difficult conditions.*

minute), about half the number (Pushkarev and Zupan, 1975). This means that London and New York design standards fall into the range classified as 'extremely restricted' (Fruin, 1971). These standards were set when such a growth in passenger movement was never considered, and at a time when financial restraints were severe. Today, it is important, particularly in the case of underground construction, that future growth is allowed for, which is so costly to provide at a later date.

## Land enhancement

In recent years there has been an increased interest by developers in the importance of rail systems in the inner city, and for stations to be integrated into new development. Scarborough, Ontario – a new retail and municipal centre – north of Toronto, is an example of this where the UTDC system, also used in Vancouver, opened in 1985 and has encouraged high-density development (Allen, 1986). London's Docklands, discussed below, is a similar story. Four different approaches are made by operating authorities and developers, to benefit financially from the prime locations of stations within central areas.

1  By using air space over stations. Ideally, this is done at the planning stage, to allow foundations and columns to be built, and to permit buildings to be built above, even after the station is open. In Hong Kong around 10 per cent of the cost of constructing the rapid-transit system was met from property development over stations.

2  By encouraging new development to be directly connected to stations. In Washington DC by 1985 there were more than 150 new buildings connected to stations and being funded by six joint development projects (Keefer, 1985).

3  Through the increased rateability of land adjoining the station. In Montreal the area up to 225 metres (250 yards) from McGill station, a typical station downtown, is defined as the 'catchment area' and a dedicated proportion of the local rates, amounting to £1.1 million ($2.12 million) a year, goes towards subsidising the rapid-transit system (Rice and Kove, 1989).

4  By providing retail outlets within, or adjoining, station concourses or subways. The rents will depend on flows generated by the station. Well-designed shops, integrated into the station's design, add interest, are useful for the public, and are profitable to the transit authority.

# LIGHT RAIL

This is a development of the conventional tram, to a much improved design. In the past trams were often removed, in favour of buses, on the grounds that they conflicted with vehicular traffic. Today that position has been reversed.The first important planning initiative for light rail occurred in 1961 in Bremen, through the work of Dr Dorfler, the city traffic engineer, who planned an 'environmental cell' system for the centre, dividing it into four quadrants bisected by a tram and bus route (Thomson, 1978), surrounded by an existing ring road. This scheme led to the pedestrianisation of one principal shopping street, shared with trams, and for all vehicular traffic to enter, and leave, the 'cells' from the ring road. Gothenburg, in the early 1970s, adopted the same principle, only here the tram route crosses the ends of a segregated pedestrian street, with adjacent stops provided, and so reduces the conflict with pedestrians. Elsewhere in the central areas of European cities two approaches are made:

1   To accept that light rail runs on streets across the centre at ground level.
2   To make it run in tunnels under the centre, ramping 4–6 per cent up to run at ground level at the perimeter, in the centre of the main roads.

In suburban areas, consideration of how the tram is integrated into the street is important. Where roads are sufficiently wide, they run as in Hanover, on a central reservation with one or two lanes of traffic on each side. Stops are normally located adjoining road junctions, with light-controlled pedestrian crossings provided, serving two stops. The light-rail vehicle is fitted with an electronic device, which automatically turns the traffic lights in the approaching vehicle's favour, except where traffic is already crossing. Light-rail routes normally cover densely populated areas, within walking distance of stations, and a route of 8–10 km (5–6 miles) from the centre is ideal, to keep journey times down to an acceptable 30 minutes. Recent experience in Europe has shown that once light rail systems are built, this has encouraged the use of public transport for both journey to work and shopping trips. Much of this is due to its often careful integration with buses. For example, in Hanover special provision is made, at remote terminal stations, for cross-platform interchange between feeder buses, equipped with the identical computerised automatic vehicle monitoring

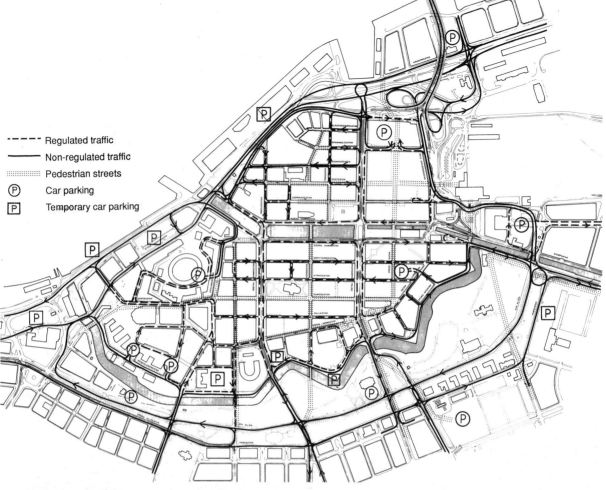

- - - - Regulated traffic
———— Non-regulated traffic
:::::::::: Pedestrian streets
Ⓟ Car parking
🄿 Temporary car parking

*Figure 115* Gothenburg, Sweden. Plan of central area (above) showing subdivision into five separate environmental zones, divided by public transport routes for trams and buses. Traffic enters for servicing or to park from the outer ring road, but cannot pass between zones. Parking is being reduced by over 2000 spaces which are to be sited further out due to improved public transport. A typical main road in Gothenburg (left) used by trams with side lanes for buses and cyclists. Photo Ekman. Courtesy Goteborgs

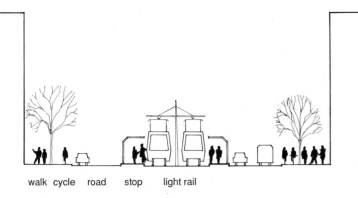

walk  cycle  road  stop  light rail

**Figures 116, 117** *Cross-section through a typical main road in Hanover showing the light rail at the centre with stops, a dual carriageway, cycle tracks and pavement. Stops are reached by passengers using light-controlled zebra crossings. The view is taken in the middle of Hanover.*
Courtesy USTRA.

*Figures 118, 119* Cross-section through a street in central Hanover, too narrow for traffic and turned into an exclusive bus and tram-only section for one block. Traffic is diverted around this.

*Figures 120a, 120b* Grenoble's principal shopping street, rue Felix Foulat, pedestrianised and repaved with a two-way tram route and access for deliveries between 6 a.m. and 1.30 p.m.

**Figure 121** *Narrow shopping street in the centre of Grenoble with tram tracks and a typical tram stop elevated to the same level as the low-slung floor of specially-built trams for wheelchair access, by ramping pavements. Access along street is also for taxis and deliveries.*

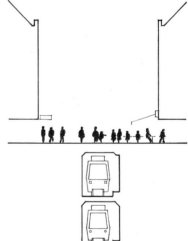

**Figures 122, 123** *Section through Listermeile, Hanover, a newly developed subcentre where because of the street width, twin tram tunnels are built above one another to avoid foundations and services to the buildings above. The street has been made pedestrian-only, paved over, trees planted and has two stations at around 500-yard intervals.*

equipment, as on the light-rail car, so that their arrival time can be co-ordinated. Hanover experienced a 46 per cent increase in the use of public transport when light rail started running (Hall and Hass-Klau, 1985). It is equally important for park-and-ride to be well connected to light rail or rapid transit. Hamburg is building five-storeyed parking for 500–1000 cars, south of the city, with direct access from each level to platform level on the S-Bahn. This is a largely political solution to counteract a demand for more parking space in the city centre.

## Technology

The vehicles used in new light-rail systems are normally articulated, two or three cars long and capable of carrying around 250 passengers, with seats for between 20 and 50 per cent of passengers. They have a high acceleration rate, can travel at speeds of 70–80 km/h (40–50 mph), with an operating speed of 20 km/h (12–15 mph), at 90-second headway, if under computer control, and with a capacity of around 15,000 passengers per hour in each direction. They can turn through a tight radius of 25 metres (85 feet), in order to run on existing streets. To achieve these speeds, stopping time at stations has to be minimal. Tickets are normally pre-bought. Suburban stops are frequently raised above ground level, approached by ramp so that cars are level with platforms for easy and quick loading, even by disabled people. Alternatively, loading is necessary from street level, and special fold-down steps are used. In Grenoble and Geneva the centre car has a low-slung floor only 34 cm (14 inches) above the railhead, for easy boarding by the ambulant disabled.

## Construction

Light rail in tunnels is frequently dimensioned to allow for a future upgrading of the system to semi-metro size, requiring a wider tunnel, and longer station platforms. Cut-and-cover construction is, however, very disruptive, although advanced methods, as used in Edmonton, Alberta, allowed tunnels to be covered in within 14 weeks (Guillot, 1983). New methods of construction, such as the 'Milan' method (Vuchic, 1981), allow tunnel roofs to be built first, and roads to be quickly reinstated. In Hanover, on Line H, two sections of tunnel built have resulted in an environmental gain. At Lister Meile, a pedestrian street was created, following the completion of a two-level tunnel below, and is served by two stations 500 metres (1/4 mile) apart. On the same line, between the interchange station Klopke, and the main line railway station, rather than replace the soil back above the twin light rail

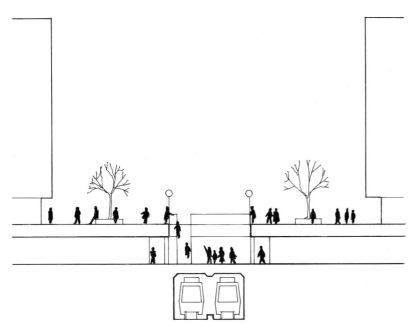

**Figures 124, 125** *Section through Bahnhofstrasse, Hanover, showing twin light-rail tunnels built two floors below ground level to provide for a mezzanine to the station linked to the main line station by a continuous low-level walkway (called the Passerelle). This provides an entry into the basement of existing stores and a segregated walkway crossing below the inner ring road.*

tunnels, a lower-level pedestrian street 12 metres (40 feet) wide has been formed, called the Passerelle, lined on both sides with shops, some of which open into the basements of large stores above. This lower level provides protection on each side from weather, and a segregated crossing below the two-way tram-only street, in front of the station. It is used by an estimated 14,000 people at peak hours, walking to the station. Servicing of the lower-level shops is from a service tunnel, connected to a peripheral road, outside the pedestrian area. These two examples show how a light railway has been closely integrated into the fabric of the existing city, and makes, through careful pre-planning, an important contribution to the environment.

Light rail is frequently used on underused railway tracks, taken over to reduce land acquisition costs. For example, in Newcastle, in north-east England, with a regional population of 1.2 million, a 56 km (25 mile) long light-rail system was opened in 1980, using 43 km (26 miles) of underused rail track, inserting new stations between the existing ones, and providing four interchanges for buses and park-and-ride. The Docklands Light Railway in London has similarly used 8 km (5 miles) of disused railway lines, elevated on reconditioned brick arches, built in 1872. The remainder of the first stage of the system, partly for reasons of the 'image' it gives to the area, is similarly elevated, on 65 metre (220 feet) span steel viaducts crossing the existing docks.

Light rail is an important new system which has been found, in the cities where they have recently been built, and properly integrated with buses, to improve the 'image' of public transport and even of the city itself. Because of their lower cost – under half that of rapid transit – when run at ground level, the construction of a more complete network is possible.

## ADVANCED LIGHT RAIL

### Val

In Europe, the principal new system developed has been Val, by Matra, with a 13.5-km (8.4-mile) long route which opened in Lille (population 195,000) in 1984. This uses driverless trains, running on rubber wheels, at an average speed of 35 km/h (21 mph), carrying 69 seated passengers with 56 standing, a capacity of 15,000 passengers per hour, with two-car trains. The cross-section is less than a Paris subway carriage in both dimensions and so tunnelling costs are, as a result, reduced. Val runs at peak hours at a $1\frac{1}{2}$ minute frequency carrying 3

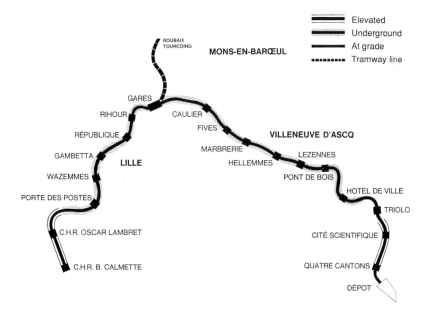

ROUBAIX
TOURCOING

MONS-EN-BARŒUL

Elevated
Underground
At grade
Tramway line

GARES

RIHOUR        CAULIER

FIVES

RÉPUBLIQUE                    VILLENEUVE D'ASCQ

MARBRERIE

GAMBETTA                    LEZENNES

LILLE        HELLEMMES

WAZEMMES                    PONT DE BOIS

PORTE DES POSTES                    HOTEL DE VILLE

TRIOLO

C.H.R. OSCAR LAMBRET

CITÉ SCIENTIFIQUE

C.H.R. B. CALMETTE        QUATRE CANTONS

DÉPOT

*Figure 126* Plan of Val rapid-transit system in Lille, France, a driverless train which runs at a frequency of 11/2 minutes, carrying around 3 million people annually. The plan indicates how 75 per cent of the 13.5 km (8.4 mile) long system runs underground across the centre.

*Figure 127* A typical station which for safety reasons has automatic sliding doors at the platform edge that open when the train comes to a stop. Courtesy Matra Transport.

**Figure 128** *Elevated section of track showing a guidance system. Cross-section of trains is substantially less than a typical Paris Métro car in order to reduce tunnelling construction costs. The system opened in 1983 and has increased public transport trips by 64 per cent. Similar systems are being planned for two other French cities. That a small city of 200,000 people have invested in such a costly system is indicative of the French commitment to public transport, and the frequency of the system and integration with buses at stations suggests what public transport could be like in all cities.*
Courtesy Matra Transport.

million people annually, and following its opening, public transport trips increased by 22 per cent. Each station is unmanned, with glazed screens, provided for reasons of safety, along the platform edge, with sliding doors which open when the train doors are exactly opposite. In the first section built, 75 per cent of the track runs in tunnel and 25 per cent is elevated. A further 10 km (6 mile) long extension opened in 1989 with 18 stations.

## UTDC (Skytrain)

Vancouver, British Columbia, with a population of 1.2 million people, following a transport plan made in 1971, planned to meet further public opposition to freeway building by restructuring its public transport system. (There is less than 1 km or 1/2 mile of freeway within the city limits). This entailed upgrading its bus and trolley car system, and the construction of Skytrain, along a 21-km (13-mile) long corridor, opened for public use in 1986. The plan is designed to reduce suburban sprawl, and slow down city centre growth by constructing sub-centres with offices, and retail shops, with high-density residential development, around stations along the route, linked to the city centre by the Skytrain system. Park-and-ride cannot be incorporated at stations, because of high land costs, but will be provided on cheap land outside when the 4 km (2.5 mile) extension is complete in 1990 (Parkinson, 1987).

The driverless, fully automated trains of two to four vehicles each, carry 40 seated and 30 standing passengers, and give a capacity range of from 5000–25,000 passengers per hour. Steel wheels are used with rubber inserts, to meet the specification of 74 dBA at 50 metres (1660 feet) with a four-car train at 80 km/h (50 mph), on elevated sections. This has been reduced in certain areas to 66 dBA, by adding noise-absorbing material, because of the dissatisfaction of residents along the route. The trains are driven by linear induction motors, and run on tracks of which 8 miles (13 km) are elevated, 3.7 miles (6 km) at grade and 1.2 miles (2 km) underground, in an existing rail tunnel. Buses act as feeders to the stations, which are unmanned.

## Kawasaki system, Port Island, Kobe

This is a fully automated system, developed by Kawasaki, the local industry, and used as the principal transport system, connecting a man-made island off the coast of Kobe, Japan, with a residential population

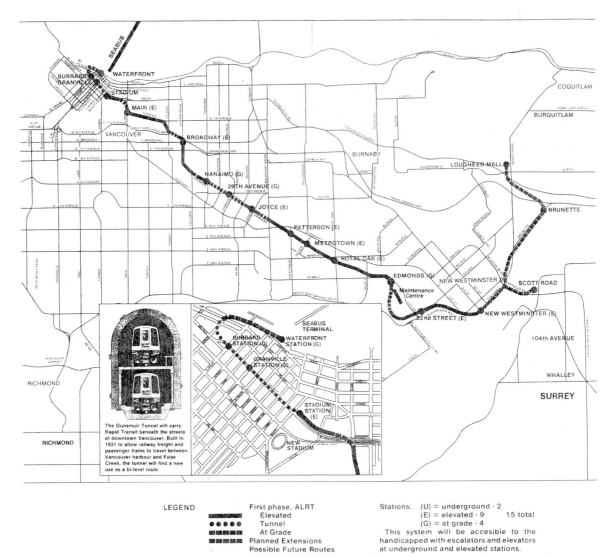

LEGEND

First phase, ALRT
Elevated
Tunnel
At Grade
Planned Extensions
Possible Future Routes

Stations: (U) = underground · 2
(E) = elevated · 9    15 total
(G) = at grade · 4
This system will be accesible to the handicapped with escalators and eievators at underground and elevated stations.

**Figure 129** *Plan of ALRT system in Vancouver, British Columbia (population 1.2 million), an elevated, driverless light-rail system 21 km (13 miles) long which has been planned to encourage growth around stations outside the central area. Park-and-ride will be concentrated at the terminal station outside the city centre and the system, together with an upgrading of public transport, is intended to remove the need for more roadbuilding.*
Courtesy Urban Transportation Development Corporation.

**Figure 130** *Section of elevated track showing two vehicle trains running on steel wheels with rubber inserts, aimed at reducing noise levels to 66 dBa in certain sections. The system is fully automated, driverless, with unmanned stations and incorporates many safety features, relying on video cameras for surveillance.*
Courtesy Urban Transportation Development Corporation.

of 22,000 people living in high rise flats, and around 40,000 people working in the business district, who need access, as commuters, to and from the main railway station, on the mainland. The system, which is entirely elevated, opened in 1981, with twelve unmanned six-car trains carrying up to 450 passengers at an average speed of 28 km/h (17 mph) over the 6.4-km (4-mile) long route. The trains carry an average of 15 million people a year.

## Docklands Light Railway, London

The closure of the docks in East London in the 1970s allowed for the redevelopment of an area, poorly served by roads and public transport. Initial proposals to extend the underground railway were likely to cost £325 million, and were rejected by the Government as too costly. Of the alternatives evaluated, a busway was rejected, in favour of light rail which was to be built for £77 million, including contingencies, elevated to give a more forward-thinking image. Completed, and running within five years, opening in 1987, this uses 8 km (5 miles) of existing railway right of way, on existing rail viaducts or at ground level, and 4 km (2–5 miles) of elevated new structure, crossing the dock basins. The trains are fully automated, each with an on-board attendant. They carry 84 seated and 126 standing passengers, and operate at service speeds of 30 km/h (19 mph) at a $7^{1}/_{2}$ minute headway.

The size of development in London's Docklands, and a decision to build Canary Wharf, one of the largest developments in Europe, has required the extension of the light railway in tunnel into the City. The length of trains and platforms are being doubled, which, with new signalling, will allow headways to be reduced to 1½ minutes, and the capacity to be increased to 15,000 passengers per hour in one direction. A 7.7 km (4.8 mile) long extension, now being built, will serve further development, paid for from the enhanced land values.

There are many systems available, often termed unconventional by transport operators, and there is a case for introducing these in situations where they can provide a useful service, principally to meet the needs of a growing number of tourists. San Francisco's cable cars are just such a system. Cities frequently have built these systems, such as the funicular in Paris, or the cable car to Roosevelt Island in New York, which are both useful and profitable, as well as adding interest to a city.

*Figure 131* *Plan of London Docklands showing 8 km (5 mile) long light railway and extensions now being built into the City of London and to the east. The system, built at a cost of £77 million, was introduced in 1987. Capacity, initially 2500 passengers per hour in one direction, is being increased to 15,000 per hour by doubling train lengths, increasing platform lengths and installing new signalling. Much of this cost is met by a private developer, and the extension east will be paid for out of enhanced land values.*
Courtesy Docklands Light Railway Ltd.

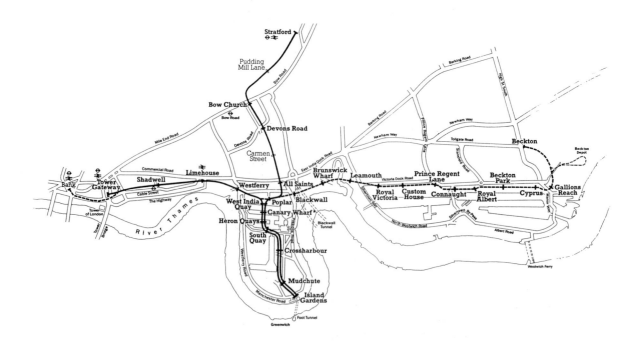

**Figure 132** *A typical station, initially designed to be extended, and now undergoing extension to allow for increased capacity. Photos and plan Docklands Light Railway.*
*The light rail system has contributed to the success of development in Docklands, where the road system will always be inadequate to meet demand. In the future with the completion of the Jubilee Line underground into Docklands, the light-railway will connect with this and serve partly as a distributor system.*
Courtesy Docklands Light Railway Ltd.

## MONORAILS

An elevated full-scale monorail was built in Seattle, Washington, in 1962 and is still running. Two were also built in Japan, where one forms a link to Haneda Airport, built in 1965 alongside a heavily congested motorway. Their only apparent advantage is that there is a slight reduction visually in the cross-section of the track seen from below, although their interest more often lies, for developers, in their 'futurist image'

A new system opened in Sydney, Australia in 1988 and connects a renewal project at Darling Harbour, with the city centre 3 km (2¼ miles) away. The monorail was chosen, over light rail, principally because it was being built by the developer without subsidy, and the state government would be given a share of the profits. The system by Von Roll/Habegger, who have built many similar ones for use in exhibition sites, is a lightweight monorail, running on an elevated steel box-section track in a single loop with five stations at a cost of $A70 million. Columns are located at around 30-metre (33-yard) centres and the cars are unmanned, under computer control, with an estimated capacity of 5500 passengers per hour.

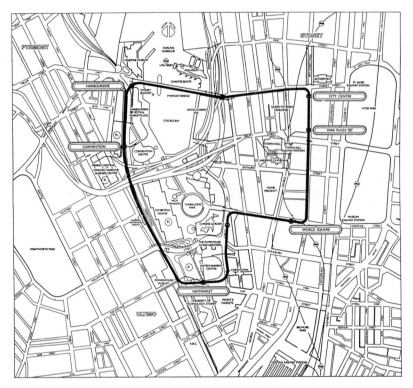

*Figure 133* Plan of 3.6-km (2-mile) long single loop monorail system which opened in 1986 in Sydney, Australia, linking the city centre to a new entertainment centre at Darling Harbour. It was built at an estimated cost of $A 70 million.
Courtesy TNT.

The visual impact on the street is minimal, although the stations are more problematic, as is the problem of walking below, or near the track in wet weather, when trains pass overhead. However, the system does seem to have much to offer for visitors, affording unique views from it of the city and the harbour development, and operates to capacity for much of the time.

**Figures 134, 135** *View of steel box-section track located above pavements. The six trains are unmanned, running under computer control. The circular stations have lift or ramp access from street to platform level, accessible for wheelchair passengers. Monorails of this kind have been built to serve many exhibitions and theme parks, and unlike the large-scale version have a reduced track dimension and slender supporting columns. No escape walkways are required from trains - fire ladders are used in the event of breakdown. This system in Sydney, much-resisted at the time it was introduced, is extremely popular, and although it is less practical for the working population than a tram, provides a useful facility for tourists.* Courtesy Heraty.

# 11
# WATER

London started a new privately operated Riverbus service in 1988, originally called Thames Line, which serves a 32-km (20-mile) long route. The service is principally designed to serve commuters from any of eight piers located between a new luxury housing development at Chelsea Harbour to Greenwich, including a stop at Docklands, where it will serve Canary Wharf, among other developments. The service is carrying around 1500 commuters a day, with boats operating seven days a week. On weekdays the service runs between 7 a.m. and 10 p.m., at weekends from 10 a.m. to 6 p.m. The minimum frequency is every 30 minutes, with an increased frequency to every 20 minutes at peak periods on weekdays. The aim is to provide a reliable service for regular commuters, principally to the West End and the City, London's business area, and to Docklands, a growing area of mixed development.

Two licensed watermen are required on each of the seven boats running, because of Port of London and Department of Transport operating regulations. Each boat contains 62 seats, is fully enclosed and heated in winter, with no standees allowed. Turnaround times are critical and can be affected by wind or the often very strong tidal conditions which exist on the River Thames. A full load can board in about three minutes and passengers can buy a ticket on the boat or a book of tickets at sales offices, or their companies provide them. One-way fares are between £1 and £4 maximum. Visual display screens are located at each pier, which is weather-protected, and each has a

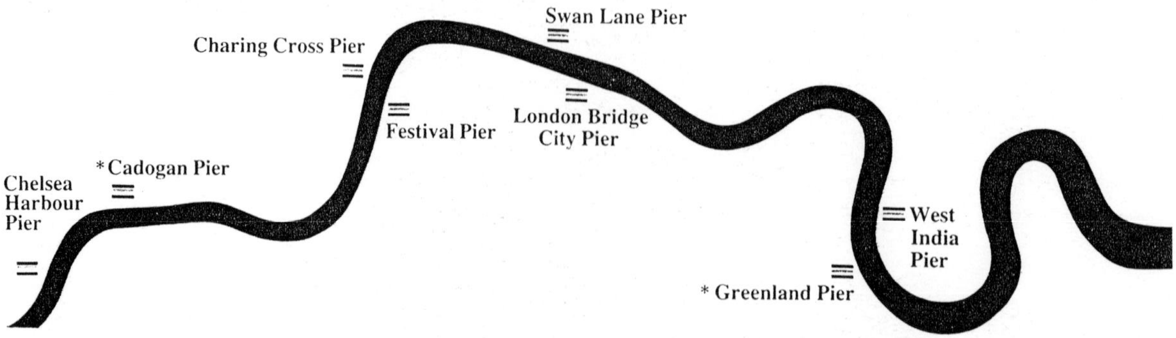

*Figure 136* Plan of Riverbus service running over a 32-km (20-mile) long route between eight piers on the River Thames, from a luxury housing scheme at Chelsea to Greenwich Pier. The service is aimed at commuters to the West End, the City and Docklands, runs seven days a week at around 15-minute intervals and carries about 1500 passengers a day.
Courtesy River Bus Partnership.

Swan Lane Pier
Charing Cross Pier
Festival Pier
London Bridge City Pier
*Cadogan Pier
Chelsea Harbour Pier
West India Pier
* Greenland Pier

**Figures 137, 138** *Boarding at a pier takes around 3 minutes and passengers can buy a book of tickets at sales offices. All eight piers are provided with screens showing real-time departure times, continually updated from the central control room. Boats carry 62 seated passengers, with no standees permitted, are operated by licensed watermen and are in radio-contact with the central control. Often severe tidal conditions have to be met on the river. London already has many tourist boats operating in the summer and in the past attempts to run commuter boats have been unsuccessful, before the growth of Docklands. Here, because of the extent of new housing and office development, a useful number of passengers already use the boats in both directions.*
Courtesy Lousada.

built-in computer, programmed to show when a boat is due in, and connected to the central control room by direct phone line. The control rooms keep in touch, directly, by radiophone with each boat, and are informed of any delays, then updating all the display screens to show any revised departure times.

Any riverbus system, to be useful in transport terms, must be easily accessible by passengers, from home or to office, and its success will also depend on the size of the catchment area and number of potential passengers it can attract from using other systems of transport. In the case of London, park-and-ride is possible at Chelsea Harbour in expensive private underground parking adjacent to the pier, but otherwise land is too valuable for a specific car park. Alternatively, space on board for cycles could be useful, but is not practical with the existing boats. Lock-up cycle parking could usefully be provided beside the piers, however, at little cost. As traffic built up, small feeder buses might prove useful, in radio contact with the control room to inform drivers of arrival times. Two feeder bus systems do in fact already serve two landing stages and more no doubt will follow in the future. The river bus service does fill a gap in London's transport network and serves areas without railways and where buses run on heavily congested roads. It provides a valuable service and in the long term may encourage more housing developments along the river banks.

# 12 CONCLUSIONS

The range of urban systems and techniques for improving movement in cities has never been so wide. All that is lacking in many cities is the courage to try them out. To summarise, then, some of the more important factors and systems which have been discussed. A positive approach to land-use planning is essential, closely related to an understanding of the role that public transport must play. An assumption by planning committees that 'everyone will drive', for example, is common, and a wrong one. Many people either don't drive, or don't have cars. This fallacy is one which has led to an acceptance of out-of-town shopping or business parks as 'what people really want', and can only lead in the long term to cities in Europe being blighted, in the same way as has happened to so many in North America. Only clear-cut policies aimed at stopping this approach, and insisting that such development occurs 'within' the city boundary or in new cities outside, will be effective.

As far as road-building is concerned, more consideration must be given to finding how the community will benefit. Roads, particularly within densely developed areas of a city, must be treated as a 'high-value' commodity and so, through tolls or pricing, new roads could be of minimum size, designed for use at peak hours by buses and freight, and so avoid the problem of their simply being used by commuter cars. Much new road-building has occurred, in the past, simply on the grounds that it was essential for the prosperity of the city. But this has never been proven. The inner ring roads, for example, built around German city centres, encourage car-commuters to drive in, until such time as the car parks are full. Now that these cities have built efficient light rail systems, these serve commuters and shoppers alike, so that this over-provision of road space was unnecessary and environmentally difficult to deal with. Essen is one example, where part of the inner ring road has now been decked over, to form a shopping area, with a bus station below, linking the city centre over the six-lane ring road with the surrounding residential area.

In Munich, the halting of the inner ring road, only part of which was built, because of public protest, has resulted in part of the outer ring being placed in tunnel, at such high cost, that any further road-building in the city has been indefinitely delayed. However, the local community, because of the high value they placed on the quality of their environment were able to insist that a solution was found regardless of cost, rather than one which would have been simply a cheaper expedient.

In terms of public transport, the bus will remain an important system and already its 'cloth-cap image' has been transformed in many cities, with newly-designed buses for easy boarding, and information systems at bus stops, to inform passengers when the bus will arrive. Some cities are investing in the infrastructure necessary for proper bus operation. Politicians will perhaps in the future be as keen to open a new length of busway as to inaugurate a new motorway. Ottawa, for example, already has a 19-mile (31-km) long 'transitway' providing a spine route for express buses which can enter at different points along the route. In Adelaide, South Australia, and Essen, West Germany, guided busways, completed and operating, could in the future be used by bus-trains, powered electrically on the track, running in tunnel below a city centre, and use non-polluting combustion engines on the roads within suburban areas. More consideration will be required to improve cross-city movement by public transport, between sub-centres outside the central area, either by bus or light rail, as an alternative to providing new roads. The scheduling system for buses in Edmonton, Alberta, has been discussed, and shows how, provided roads are sufficiently free from congestion, to allow the buses to run on time, cross-city movement can be served by public transport, and not only by car. However, local planning authorities would have to ensure that car traffic is restrained, as is being tried in California, by requiring potential developers to provide incentives for car and van-pooling, and to issue 'Travelcards' to employees, to encourage them to use public transport, instead of providing them with company cars.

Light rail systems will increasingly be built to serve the more heavily used transport corridors, in conjunction with feeder buses to stops, particularly where it is politically expedient to improve access to a central area, where there is room for increased growth. Such 'fixed track' systems are attractive to developers, because of the higher land values close to stations, or stops, and they should be obliged to contribute to their cost, as has occurred in London's Docklands. Cities, such as Vancouver, have used light rail, in this case a driverless, automated system, as part of their planning strategy, aimed at encouraging new development to occur at sub-centres around stations, rather than in the central area. Moreover, car parking is being restricted at these points because of high land values, and will be placed at the

**Figure 139** Broadgate in the City of London. A successful example of office development forming an important public space which has proved well-used for lunchtime concerts in the summer and for skating in the winter, providing a place where pedestrians can escape from streets where traffic dominates.
Photo Peter Cook. Courtesy Arup Associates-Architects Engineers Quantity Surveyors.

periphery of the city, to avoid the need for any more new roads within the city boundary.

Hamburg has already adopted a similar strategy, using its S-Bahn railway to serve peripheral park-and-ride points, and will allow no additional parking within the city centre boundary.

However, further measures in many cities will be necessary to restrain traffic at certain times of day, both entering and crossing the centre. In smaller cities, as in Florence, certain classes of vehicle will be banned or in larger cities priced, to ensure that drivers pay the cost of the congestion they cause. Singapore has been discussed, where a cordon has been made around the centre and a daily charge made to all cars, except those carrying three or more passengers. At the same time, a new rapid-transit system and a new fleet of buses have been provided. Rapid developments in 'smart-card' technology, now used at toll bridges in the United States and Norway, will in the future be used to charge drivers entering a central area, or toll road, at certain times of day, and, through the level of the charge, to restrain the numbers of vehicles entering, as well as provide an important revenue for improving public transport and the environment.

Finally, following such measures of restraint on traffic, through pricing, it will be possible for authorities to make a more concerted effort to improve the environment. With the freeing of some road space it will be easier for more streets to be closed to traffic (London has but a handful), for pavements to be widened, more trees planted, and for more residential areas to be freed from through traffic.

The means are there, the appropriate technologies have been tried and tested. What is now needed is political will, courage...and commitment.

# REFERENCES

## 1 Transport and the City

Cervero, R. (1984) 'Managing the traffic impacts of suburban office growth'. *Transportation Quarterly*, Vol. 38, No. 4, October.

Hamer, N. (1987) *Wheels within Wheels*. Routledge and Kegan Paul, London.

Kinsman, F. (1987) *The Telecommuters*. John Wiley, London.

Leavitt, H. (1970) *Superhighway – Superhoax*. Doubleday, New York.

Mogridge, M.J.H. (1985) *Jam Yesterday, Jam Today and Jam Tomorrow*. University College, London.

Mogridge, M.J.H. (1987) *A Strategic Transportation Plan for Inner East London*. Docklands Forum, 192 Hanbury St, London E1.

OECD (1974) *Streets for People: Norwich* by A.A. Wood. Organisation for Economic Co-operation and Development, 2 rue André-Pascal, 75775, Paris Cedex 16, France.

OECD (1988) *Cities and Transport*. Organisation for Economic Co-operation and Development, 2 rue André-Pascal, 75775, Paris Cedex 16, France.

Orski, K. (1987) 'Managing suburban traffic congestion: a strategy for suburban mobility'. *Transportation Quarterly*, Vol. 41, October.

Plowden, S. (1980) *Taming Traffic*. André Deutsch, London, p. 50.

Roth, G. (1967) *Paying for Roads*. Penguin, London, p. 140.

Simpson, B. (1988) 'Local public transport systems in Britain, France and Germany'. *Traffic Engineering and Control*, May, pp. 288–293.

Stewart, J.R. (1979) 'User response to pedestrianised shopping streets'. *Research Memo* 73, Centre for Urban and Regional Studies, University of Birmingham.

Stewart, G. and Mihalcin, E. (1983) 'The walk to work trip in Downtown Toronto'. *Transportation Quarterly*, Vol. 37 No. 4, October, pp. 623–633.

UMTA (1979) *Streets for Pedestrians and Transit. Transit Malls in US*. Report Urban Mass Transport Administration-MA-06-0049-79-1. National Technical Information Service, Springfield, Virginia 22161.

## 2 Walking

Hass-Klau, C. (1989) 'International experience of traffic calming: the solution to British transport problems', Traffex '89 Conference, Brighton.

Lovemark, O. (1970) 'New Approaches to Pedestrian Problems', *Transportation Systems for Major Activity Centres*. Organisation for Economic Co-operation and Development, 2 rue André-Pascal, 75775, Paris Cedex 16, France.

Pushkarev, B. and Zupan, J. (1975) *Urban Space for Pedestrians*. MIT Press, Cambridge, Mass. and London.

Robertson, K.A. (1988) 'Pedestrian skywalk systems'. *Transportation Quarterly* Vol. 42 No. 3, July, pp. 457–484.

UMTA (1979) *Streets for Pedestrians and Transit. Transit Malls in the US*. Report UMTA-MA-06-0049-79-1. National Technical Information Service, Springfield, Virginia 22161.

Whyte, W.H. (1980) *The Social Life of Small Urban Spaces*. The Conservation Foundation, 1717 Massachusetts Avenue NW, Washington DC 20036.

## 3 Mobility for Elderly and Disabled People

ECMT (1988) 'Transport for disabled people and cars'. European Conference of Ministers of Transport. Organisation for Economic Co-operation and Development, 2 rue André Pascal, 75775 Paris Cedex 16, France.

ECMT (1987) 'Transport for disabled people. Developing accessible transport: the role of demand-responsive services'. ECMT Seminar, 1986. Organisation for Economic Co-operation and Development, 2 rue André Pascal, 75775 Paris Cedex 16, France.

Heraty, M.J. (1989) Paper presented at proceedings of 5th international conference on mobility and transport for elderly and disabled people in developing countries. Swedish Board of Transport Box 1339 S-171 26 Solna, Stockholm.

Oxley, P.R. (1988) 'Disabled people and cars: an overview'. ECMT Seminar, April 1988.

US DOT (1980) 'Development of priority accessible networks'. *Provisions for the Elderly and Handicapped Pedestrians*. US Department of Transportation, Federal Highway Administration, Contract. DOT-FH-11-8504, Washington DC.

## 4 Cycling

Grabe, W. and Utech, J. (1984) 'The importance of the bicycle in local public passenger transport'. *UITP Revue*, No. 3, pp. 246–255.

Hudson, M. (1982) *Bicycle Planning. Policy and Practice*. Architectural Press, London.

Jun Meng Yang (1985) 'Bicycle traffic in China'. *Transportation Quarterly*, Vol. 39 No. 1, January, pp. 93–107.

Replogle, M.A. (1983) *Bicycle Access to Public Transportation. Urban Transport Abroad*. CIVL, 818 18th St NW, Washington DC 20006.

## 5 The Car

May, A.D. (1986) 'Traffic restraint: a review of the alternatives'. *Transportation Research*, Vol. 20A No. 2, pp. 109–121.

Mogridge, M.J.H. (1985) 'The use of rail transport to improve accessibility in large conurbations'. *Town Planning Review*, Vol. 58 No. 2, pp. 165–182.

*National Travel Survey 1985/86* (1988) *An Analysis of Personal Travel*. HM Stationery Office, London.

Orski, K.C. (1988) 'Traffic mitigation and developers', March, Urban Land Institute, 1090 Vermont Ave NW, Washington DC 2005.

Plowden, S. (1980) *Taming Traffic*. André Deutsch, London, pp. 77–79.

TEST (1984) *The Company Car Factor*. TEST, 177 Arlington Road, London NW1 7EY.

Wohl, M. (1976) 'The present role of taxis in urban America'. *The Taxi Project. Catalogue*. Museum of Modern Art, New York.

World Bank (1984) *Singapore Area Licensing Scheme. A Review of the Impact,* by Pendakur and Armstrong-Wright. World Bank, Washington DC.

## 6 Road Pricing and Controls

Borins, S.F. (1988) 'Electronic road pricing: an idea whose time may never come'. *Transportation Research*, Vol. 22A, pp. 37–44.

Fong, P.K.W. (1985) 'Issues of the electronic road pricing system in Hong Kong'.

*Transportation Planning and Technology,* Vol. 10. Gordon and Breach, London.

GLC (1974) *Area Control: a Scheme for Reducing Car Traffic in Central London, to Limit Congestion and Improve the Environment.* Greater London Council, London.

LPAC (1989) *Desk Study: Road User Charges.* MVA Consultancy. London Planning Advisory Committee, Eastern House, 8–10 Eastern Road, Romford, Essex.

Roth, G. (1967) *Paying for Roads.* Penguin, London.

World Bank (1984) *Singapore Area Licensing Scheme. A Review of the Impact.* Pendakur and Armstrong-Wright, World Bank, Washington DC.

## 7 Freight

Collins, M.F. and Pharoah, T.M. (1974) *Transport Organisation in a Great City.* Allen and Unwin, London.

Plowden, S. (1980) *Taming Traffic.* André Deutsch, London, pp. 147–153.

TRRL (1973) *Urban Freight Distribution: a Study of Operations in High St, Putney.* A.W. Christie and J. Prudhoe. Transport and Road Research Laboratory, Crowthorne, Berkshire, UK. Report LR556.

TRRL (1976) *Design and Cost of a Trans-shipment depot to Serve Swindon Town Centre.* J. Battilana and I. Hawthorne. Transport and Road Research Laboratory, Crowthorne, Berkshire, UK. Report 741.

TRRL (1979) *Quiet Vehicle Programme.* J. Tyler. Transport and Road Research Laboratory, Crowthorne, Berkshire, UK. Report SR5218.

## 8 Buses

Turner, R.P. and White, P.R. (1987) *NBC's urban minibuses: a review and financial appraisal.* Transport and Road Research Laboratory, Crowthorne, Berkshire, UK. Contractor's Report 42.

White, P. (1986) *Public Transport: Its planning, Management and Operation.* Hutchinson Educational. London, pp.52–54.

## 9 Interchanges

Bell, M.C. (1976) 'Passenger transport interchange: a state of the art review'. University of Newcastle upon Tyne, Department of Civil Engineering, Division of Transport Engineering, Newcastle upon Tyne, UK. Transport Operations Research Group, Report 10.

Bixby, B. (1986) *Integration in Transport. The Role of Park-and-Ride.* Oxford Polytechnic Department of Town Planning, Working Paper 92, July.

Cervero, R. (1986) 'Urban transit in Canada. Integration and innovation at its best'. *Transportation Quarterly*, Vol. 40 No. 3, July.

Grabe, W. and Utech, J. (1984) 'The importance of the bicycle in local public passenger transport'. *UITP Revue*, No. 3, pp. 246–255.

LPAC (1989) *Desk Study: Road User Charges.* MVA Consultancy. London Planning Advisory Committee, Eastern House, 8–10 Eastern Road, Romford, Essex.

OECD (1988) *Cities and Transport.* Organisation for Economic Co-operation and Development, 2 rue André-Pascal, 75775, Paris Cedex 16, France.

Sheldon, R. (1985) 'Real time bus arrival information'. *Seminar J*, July. PTRC Education and Research Services, Glenthorne House, Hammersmith Grove,

London W6.

Turner, F.P.S. (1959) 'Preliminary planning for a new tube railway across London'. *Proceedings of the Institution of Civil Engineers*, London, No. 12, pp. 19–38.

Toronto Transit Commission (1988) *Corporate Policy Document on Commuter Parking*. April,. TTC, 1900 Yonge St, Toronto, Canada.

Wagon, D.J. and Collins, P.H. (1973) 'Influence of cost, quality and organisation of terminal transport and interchanges'. *Report on the 19th Round Table on Transport Economics*. European Conference of Ministers of Transport, Paris.

## 10  Rail

Allen, J.G. (1986) 'Public-private joint development at rapid transit stations'. *Transportation Quarterly*, Vol. 40 No. 3, July, pp. 317–331.

Fruin, J.J. (1971) *Pedestrian Planning and Design*. MAUDEP, PO Box 722, Church St Station, New York, NY 10008.

Guillot E. (1983) 'LRT design choices – Edmonton and Calgary'. *Transportation Quarterly*. Vol. 37 No. 3, July, pp. 337–354.

Hall, P. (1980) *Great Planning Disasters*. Penguin, London, pp. 109–137.

Hall, P. and Hass-Klau, C. (1985) *Can Rail Save the City*? Gower Press, Farnborough, Hampshire.

Keefer, L.F. (1985) 'Joint development at US transit stations'. *Transportation* No. 12, pp. 333–342.

Parkinson, T. (1987) 'Skytrain in Vancouver, Canada'. *UITP Revue* No. 3.

Rice, R.G. and Kove, T. (1989) *Public/Private Sector Financing Techniques for Urban Transit in Canada*. School of Urban Planning, McGill University, Montreal.

Pushkarev, B. and Zupan, P. (1975) *Urban Spaces for Pedestrians*. MIT Press, Cambridge, Mass. and London.

Vuchic, V.R. (1981) *Urban Public Transportation*. Prentice-Hall, New Jersey.

# INDEX

*References to figure numbers are in
bold type*